£1

WORKING WITH GROUPS

D0120800

Psychology

Editor

PROFESSOR GEORGE WESTBY

Professor of Psychology, University College of South Wales, Cardiff

WORKING WITH GROUPS

THE SOCIAL PSYCHOLOGY OF
DISCUSSION AND DECISION

Josephine Klein

Director, Community and Youth Work Course,
Goldsmiths' College, University of London

HUTCHINSON UNIVERSITY LIBRARY
LONDON

HUTCHINSON & CO (*Publishers*) LTD
178–202 Great Portland Street, London W1

London Melbourne Sydney
Auckland Johannesburg Cape Town
and agencies throughout the world

First published 1961
Second edition (Revised) 1963
Reprinted 1966, 1968, 1970

Printed in Great Britain by litho on smooth wove paper
by Anchor Press, and bound by Wm. Brendon,
both of Tiptree, Essex

ISBN 0 09 062463 7 (cased)
0 09 062464 5 (paper)

CONTENTS

ACKNOWLEDGMENTS

I take this opportunity to acknowledge my gratitude to the many students on whom these theories were first tried out, especially to those who provided the examples on pages 87 and 89–99 by writing essays on social relations in organizations with which they were familiar, and to those who provided the interaction-sequence examples for the final three chapters. I am also grateful to my colleague, Dr Winifred Cavenagh, for many discussions and for the formulation of the questions reproduced on pages 82–5.

I should like to thank Nigel Balchin and William Collins Sons & Co. Ltd for permission to quote from *Sundry Creditors*; R. F. Bales for permission to quote from *Interaction Process Analysis*; E. A. Bennett and Tavistock Publications for permission to quote from 'Discussion, decision, commitment and consensus in group decision' in *Human Relations* VIII; Arthur Koestler and Jonathan Cape Ltd for permission to quote from *Darkness at Noon*; D. Krech and D. Crutchfield and McGraw-Hill Book Co. Inc. for permission to quote from *Theory and Problems in Social Psychology*; R. Lippitt and Harper and Brothers for permission to quote from *Training in Community Relations*; M. L. K. Pringle and the Editors of the *Educational Review* for permission to quote from 'An experiment in parent-staff group discussion'; Jeanne Watson and the American Sociological Association for permission to quote from 'A formal analysis of social interaction' in *Sociometry*

ACKNOWLEDGMENTS

XXI; G. Wilson and G. Ryland and Houghton Mifflin Co. for permission to quote from *Social Group Work Practice*; and Alvin Zander and Tavistock Publications for permission to quote from 'The W.P. Club: an objective case study of a group' in *Human Relations* I.

INTRODUCTORY

THIS introduction is intended to provide a summary of the argument pursued in the subsequent chapters. In order to do this as clearly as possible, the theory on which the argument is based must first be briefly outlined.

Working with groups requires three skills: an understanding of theory, a knowledge of its application, and trained experience in its use. The first of these skills, an understanding of theory, is the most certain means to appropriate application and effective practice. But this is only so if the theory is *operational*: it must be closely linked to the categories by which the group can be observed and analysed. The discussion of theory in this chapter will therefore be in terms of the categories of interaction according to which events in the group can be classified. These are: information, views, proposals, agreement, and individual self-expression.

At its best, the process of interaction moves regularly through an identifiable sequence of phases. Briefly: in order to make a decision a group needs to have the fullest possible *information*, on the basis of which *views* are expressed and *proposals* made, until finally one proposal manages to secure *agreement* from the majority of those present. This process is, however, frequently interrupted by the intrusion of the private preoccupations of members of the group.

What are these private preoccupations? They stem from the fact that a group member is also an individual person, with his own values, motives, and goals. Because these are important to him, an unskilled member may intrude them on the group when he should not, as well as when he may.

This leads to the second main point of the argument. It is

possible to define the circumstances in which *self-expression* is appropriate and to distinguish these from the circumstances in which it is inappropriate.

Some kinds of self-expression are relevant to the values and goals which individuals wish to pursue as members of the group. These find utterance in the views which the individual contributes to the group, when the information at the group's disposal is commented upon and organized in such a way that the individuals' goals and the group's goals are compatible. There is thus a value-element in the expression of an individual's views which is absent from the factual giving of information. This element is stronger still when he makes a proposal, and essential to his agreement with the group's decision. When he engages in this kind of self-expression he is contributing to the performance of the group's task: it is therefore appropriate.

Other kinds are irrelevant to the values and goals which the members of the group wish to pursue. As far as furthering the task in a direct way is concerned, these are better not uttered. Nevertheless, they often serve a cohesive function: improving the morale and self-satisfaction of the group.

The theory can be summarized in a little diagram:

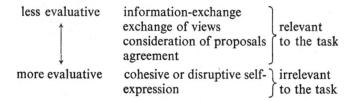

The arrangement of the chapters will now be seen to follow a reasonable pattern. Following this introductory chapter, there will be a discussion of some other types of interaction-analysis, and of the difficulties encountered in their construction and use. Conveniently, this discussion provides a broad, though superficial, survey of the kind of material with which the study of groups is concerned.

Chapters 3 and 4 are designed to establish the theoretical framework and to give practice in the identification of the interaction-categories. Both these chapters will be mainly concerned with interaction relevant to the performance of a task. To restore the balance, chapters 5 and 6 deal exclusively with the self-expressive side of interaction, first from the point of view of the individual, his motives and satisfactions; then from the point of view of the group, its structure and its cohesion. It may be thought that these two chapters are a shade too psychological, concentrating on considerations of personality-development and irrationality. I believe, however, that they are a necessary corrective, which may prevent facile misinterpretations of a book whose main emphasis is on the improvement, by rational techniques, of habitual reactions when working with groups.

Thereupon the theoretical framework is taken for granted, and the subsequent chapters, on the social context within which a group operates, on leadership, structure, function, and morale, and on the possibility of changing ideas through group action, represent an attempt to apply the more rigorous approach of the social scientist to the complex situations so characteristic of the subject-matter. These are applied chapters: they use the theory outlined in the earlier analysis to deal with practical considerations. Part of this section is very down-to-earth indeed, reviewing, for instance, committee-procedure in the light of laboratory findings on discussion-groups. The recommendations arising out of this review may not prove easily acceptable: 'This would double the time spent in committees!' 'How would we ever get anything done?' I hope, however, that these criticisms will come to be recognized as invalid. Bad habits in any skill enable a man to 'get along', but they prevent him from reaching perfect competence. If his performance is to be improved, a period of re-training is necessary, and during this time he will necessarily be slower than he would otherwise have been. Anyone knows this who has taught a child to swim well. But when eventually the committee-members have learnt to pare their proceedings down to essentials, they will take much less time than before. They will gain in efficiency and morale, and be more democratic into the bargain. Chapter 11, which consists of two lengthy records of meetings and a running commentary on them, may help to persuade those who have doubts on the value of training.

The final section—chapters 12, 13, and 14—is devoted to training for an improvement of interaction. This is in a way an impossible task to set oneself when writing a book. How can one interact with one's readers? But learning to work with groups cannot indefinitely be restricted to paperwork. It was felt that some attempt must be made to provide practical experience for those who wanted it. This is the aim of the three training chapters. The first two are designed to give the student experience of the difficulties encountered when attempting to conform to an ideal outline in a real-life situation; the last is intended to enable him to recognize the difficulties the group at work will encounter, while he himself is actually involved in the group and its work. The problem of presentation has been solved to some extent by creating the fiction that the book is addressed to small groups of readers who are willing to put their ideas into practice by participating in the training situations known technically as 'role-playing groups'.

This fiction produced another difficulty, since it is likely that not only the notion of membership in a role-playing group, but even more the responsibility of leadership in such a group, is unfamiliar to most readers. It is the task of the leader or instructor of a role-playing group to create an atmosphere in which members feel free to make mistakes as they try out rather more efficient techniques than those they are in the habit of using. These final three chapters are there-fore designed, in so far as is possible, to help both an inex-perienced instructor and the group in which he works. This has had to be done at the expense of good writing. Basically, however, these techniques are not very difficult to grasp in-tellectually, and once a glimpse has been caught of how the process works, most instructors should be able to develop the style most congenial to them.

Finally, it may be as well to deal here with another objection to this kind of work. I have found that a resistance to comprehension and learning arises at the point when the student first realizes he is getting the hang of the thing. He feels reluctant to lose his psychological naïveté. He says that he would rather lose his case by honest means than gain it by Machiavellian ones. This objection is based on a misunderstanding (as well as on the fact that he has often had no experience of losing cases which he very much wanted to win). The training aims at the widest possible information-exchange, and the clearest exposition of possibly incompatible values, this process continuing until agreement can be reached. As in any other game of skill, if all the players of this game are 'honest', training enables them to recognize irrelevances and not to waste time on them. If some of the players are 'dishonest', consciously or unconsciously, they cannot win except on good factual grounds if the others know the game. If one has seen the game played with 'dishonest' players, one cannot fail to be struck by the ease with which their (largely unconscious) wiles can be circumvented within the rules of the game. Awareness of the rules has no moral significance, either for honesty or dishonesty; it simply makes the game worth playing.

2

WHAT HAPPENS IN GROUPS:
THE DISADVANTAGES OF OBSERVATION
WITHOUT THEORY

Not every event can be perceived or recorded. Observation of events in groups depends on a conscious or unconscious evaluation of their significance. Observation-schedules should therefore always be based on explicit theories of group-events. Equally, theories should be capable of verification by means of an appropriate observation-schedule.

SOME years ago two psychologists wrote to all those who had been present at a meeting of the British Psychological Society and asked them what they could remember of the recent discussion. Upon analysis, it was found that only about a tenth of the points that had been made were recalled in the reports. Of these, nearly half were 'substantially incorrect'. Both logical and emotional factors had led the members of the Society to recall events which had never happened, and further distortions were due to omissions, exaggerations, or plain muddleheadedness. On the average, a member recalled about three times as many of his own points as points made by other people. The average member was, however, no more accurate about himself than he was about others.

This little anecdote illustrates the kind of problem which faces those concerned with the development of the social sciences. The layman who has a little knowledge of the physical sciences takes it for granted that techniques of observation and measurement are somehow 'given', obvious and inescapable: judgments of distance, size, weight, and colour are drummed into us so that we come to believe (mistakenly, by the way) that we think naturally in these categories. But categories of observation and measurement in the social sciences have not yet developed to the point where they become part of our thinking, not even of the thinking of social scientists, as the anecdote shows.

More embarrassing still, it has taken a while for social scientists to realize that this difficulty exists. One reason for this delay is that there are different kinds of social scientists, and each kind was able to solve its own problems temporarily to its own satisfaction. In this chapter three types of solution will be looked at and commented upon. By this means, a second purpose is also served: the student is granted a glimpse of the wealth of events which are properly the subject-matter of small-group studies.

1 The practical worker with groups: trained introspection and recall

In numerous professions, people spend their time working with groups: managing them, helping them, exploiting them, discussing with them. They vary in the skill with which they do this, and the better ones have accumulated from experience their own (possibly unconscious) categories of observation and analysis. They are able to react to what is happening in the group as is most expedient. A social worker, for instance, has to observe what is happening and evaluate its significance in relation to the possibilities it offers of improving members' behaviour, either individually or in their interaction with one another. He will tend to focus on those events which indicate possible means of improvement. A good example of the kind of considerations he may be expected to keep in mind comes from Wilson and Ryland (1949):

> The worker makes 'on the spot' analyses which immediately change his procedure with the group. He makes 'hind-sight' analyses as he writes his records and thinks through the last session. He remembers and sees the events of the meeting and the members' reactions in a little

different light and he finds new leads for programme, related to the needs of the members and the group-as-a-whole. For example, as he thinks through the comments of the members on the suggestion that they have a cook-out in the park, he suddenly remembers that Johnny said nothing. He wonders about this and remembers that Johnny once said he always had to be home by five o'clock so that his mother could go to work downtown. At the next meeting the worker makes a point of discovering if all the members are free to go on a supper cook-out or whether a Saturday lunch would not be better.

Or, as he writes his records, he comments on the *esprit de corps* and unusual degree of co-operation. Looking at the names of the members he has listed as present, he discovers that Bill's name is missing. This makes him wonder if in the past Bill has quietly and effectively blocked the programme plans of the group. Or the exact opposite may be true: the group was restless and discouraged; perhaps Bill is the person who holds it together. Points like these are often not noticed until the worker thinks through what he will put in the record.

In general, the worker should be able to find, in his record, material which throws light on the following questions in relation to programme:

Is the group interested in programme planning? Do the members feel that they are the ones who determine what they are going to do? Or is their interest only in the rough and tumble play of the moment, with acceptance of whatever the worker or any member proposes? How was the programme planned? By the worker, one individual member, a small group, a committee, the whole group? Is the planning done through informal conversation, discussion, reports of committees, parliamentary procedure? Is the method of programme planning in keeping with what may be expected from the age and social development of the members? Who suggests what? Who approves or rejects the idea? Is there any relation between the status of the member who makes the suggestion and the acceptance or rejection of the idea by others? Is there an alignment of subgroups in this process?

What is the reaction of individual members as they participate in the activities? How are they fitting the activities to their needs? When teams are chosen, who are the captains? Who is chosen on what team? Who is chosen first? Last? Do some members have status while engaging in some activities, and little when any other programme-content is uppermost? Do subgroups stand out in team-play? Is winning important to some and not to others? To what extent is the morale of the group related to the particular form of the programme? Is there real interest in the activity?

How does a certain idea, later developed by the whole group, originate? What are the 'germs' of ideas for possible future programmes?

Wilson and Ryland devote more than a hundred pages to reproductions of actual records made by workers with children, adults, the aged, and people in special circumstances. These are well worth looking at. Clearly those trained by the authors will miss very little of significance. Equally clearly, Wilson and Ryland are teaching an art, not a science: the worker's performance depends on insight rather than on systematic knowledge of interaction-processes. This means that training will be of greater benefit to the outstanding than to the ordinary student, who needs it more.

2 *The experimental worker with groups: an observation-schedule*

As well as social workers, there are research workers interested in small groups. In so far as their approach is systematic, it has a bearing on the problem of how to teach the ordinary student of social work. Research workers have tended to be of two kinds. Some, with whom we shall deal in the third section of this chapter, have tended to be primarily concerned with constructing interaction-schedules which will make observation of behaviour in groups simpler, more accurate, and easier to recall. Others have been primarily concerned with observing what happens in groups in order to make generalizations about such processes as 'leadership', 'decision-making' or 'attitude-changes', and their observation-schedules are geared to their interests. A good representative of this latter set is Alvin Zander's *Adult-Youth Participation Sheet*, which may also be regarded as an attempt to overcome the drawbacks of Wilson and Ryland's approach.

Zander leaves little to chance or choice, formulating a clear, tidy scheme which seems foolproof in the sense that any untrained person could use it. It represents a conscious attempt to classify information about group-events in such a way that it can be used for comparative purposes by others interested in similar types of groups. In this respect it may be thought both an advance on Wilson and Ryland's technique and a step to further their aims, for the tidier the scheme, the more easily it is understood and remembered, and the better it is adapted to teaching purposes.

Comparing Wilson and Ryland's list with that of Zander's, the former does appear impressionistic and untidy. The lay-out of the questions is partly responsible for this, as is also the absence of technical phrases and the assumption that the observer knows what the writer is talking about. Zander imitates more closely the objective methods of science.

The impression of tidiness is, however, deceptive. It is like a tidy kitchen-shelf on which cocoa, cups, a couple of cookbooks, and a cauliflower have been neatly arranged. There is good reason why these should all be in the kitchen (it is indeed an excellent schedule for certain purposes) but no reason why they should be there, all together on the same shelf.

For the sake of brevity a number of the items from Zander's *Adult-Youth Participation Sheet* are here omitted. The observer is expected to tick off those events which have occurred every five minutes, using a new set of papers on each occasion.

15. Who is in charge? . . . youth . . . adult.

16. Style of adult influence (act-profiles): (draw lines connecting appropriate aspects of the activity).

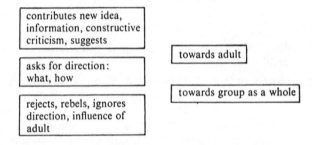

17. Style of child or youth participation (act-profiles): (draw lines connecting appropriate aspects of the activity).

reinforces child or group direction

no autonomy of reaction implied

action towards individual child

initiates direction for child or group

autonomy of reaction implied

action towards total group

changes direction for child or group

autonomy of reaction stated, invited, stimulated

stops, forbids, interrupts direction

contributes new idea, information, constructive criticism, suggests

towards adult

asks for direction: what, how

towards group as a whole

rejects, rebels, ignores direction, influence of adult

Pattern of group transitions

18. Group style of starting, stopping, changing activities (check each occurrence):

... Start, stop, or change in group activity brought about by idea of adult as to what is now most desirable or proper or appropriate thing to do (may be a prearranged programme by leader, or spur of the moment, but not in minds of group members beforehand).

... Start, stop, or change called for by prearranged programme known to group members through knowledge of pre-planning.

... Start, stop, or change called for by group tradition as to timing, sequence of activities, etc.

... Start, stop, or change due to ideas emerging from group at the time as to what is most desirable, proper, or appropriate to do.

Transmission of ideology—style and content

19. Anecdotes number 1, 2, 3, etc.

(The following material should be used separately for each anecdote occurring during observation time unit):

(a) way adult introduces ideology item to child or group (check) should do ..., should not do ..., should know ..., should not know ..., ought to do ..., ought not to do ..., a good thing ..., a bad thing ..., praises for ..., criticizes for ...

(b) describe what adult is trying to 'put across' to the child or group ...

(c) source of standard indicated in adult statement or appeal or action: appeal to higher authority ..., adult's own standards ..., 'what other people think' ..., the code of the child group ..., appeal to 'rights' of others ..., appeal to institutional or organizational standards ..., other ...

Group activity during this time unit

20. Purpose of group activity being observed (check):

fun, recreational, social ...

learning, education ...

organizing, administration ...

being 'motivated', pep talk, ritual . . .
routines, chores, 'duties' . . .
others . . .

21. Specifically, what are they doing? . . .

22. Method of participation in the activity by the group (check):
   . . . practising, drill, trying out
   . . . game, contest, competing
   . . . listening, looking
   . . . being tested, quizzed
   . . . discussion
   . . . creating, studying, making
   . . . other

23. Differentiation of function for participants in this activity (check one):
   . . . the activity is of a type where everyone in the group is doing the same thing in the same way.
   . . . the activity is made up of several different functions for different subgroups of the total group.
   . . . every participant has a unique function in this activity.

24. 'Creativity potential' of the activity (check one):
   . . . the activity and materials are of such a nature that the part being played by most of the participants is pretty much routine; little opportunity for creative invention—only one way to do it.
   . . . the activity and materials as being conducted allow considerable opportunity for the participant to invent, create, have ideas, etc.

25. Functional group structure in the present activity (check one):
   . . . everybody is 'on his own'; no mutual dependence on other participants; anybody could drop out without making much difference to rest of group.
   . . . members not depending on each other, but everyone has to do his particular job in order that a total job is to be done; they are co-ordinated as cogs in an

assembly-line fashion; but everyone is doing his own part of the job pretty much by himself.

... there is a high degree of mutual interdependence in the carrying on of the activity; each contributing in interacting fashion.

26. Adult-group interaction pattern (check one):

... all adult behaviour is coming from group members, directed toward the adult.

... all behaviour is from the adult, directed toward the group, or members.

... adult takes up about half of the total social interaction, about as much as all the other group members put together.

... adult's social acts about as frequent as average group member.

... adult definitely a peripheral member in the interaction pattern of the group.

27. The 'etiquette of communication' used in this group (check one):

... every member just talks when he feels like it, either to the whole group or to neighbours; considerable confusion and competition for attention results.

... everyone speaks up informally when he feels like it, but no disorder results; everyone seems to listen or speak in proper place with due respect to others with no special rules of recognition being necessary.

... everyone signals the adult or person in charge for recognition before he speaks, but air is quite informal (what signal . . .)

... speaking is done only when called on. Person in charge may ask for signals as to who wants to be called on, but it is definitely a 'calling on' process rather than spontaneous demanding right to speak.

28. Intensity of interest in group activity (check one):

... extreme lack of interest—group literally turn backs on activity, wander away, daydream, horseplay, call it 'quits'.

... boredom with some social restraint to expressing it actively, yawning, whispering, looking around but still some pretence of being 'in the situation' of the activity.

... signs of mild lack of interest—smothered yawning, head and leg twisting, eye wandering.

... signs of mild positive interest—relaxed attention, relatively few excursions away from activity.

... attentive interest, concentration—active interest shown by posture or actions, interest actively focused on the activity.

... enthusiastic interest—entering into activity with all energy and spirit, clear enthusiasm for activity, all-out participation.

Schedules such as these are very fascinating to read through and appear remarkably complete in detail, but they are hard to remember and generally loose in texture. This is typical of the early attempts at schedule-construction. When little was known about the systematic relationships between group-events, a happy-go-lucky approach was quite justified. Someone might wonder how many kinds of leadership there were, think up some possible varieties, watch a group of children and tick off an item on his list whenever the kind of behaviour he had in mind occurred. Or someone might note every time a new idea or a new activity is started in the group, or every time somebody is rude to somebody else, or nice to him, and explain why he thought it happened that way. Simply writing down who talked with whom, and for how long, was discovered to be a surprisingly fruitful technique. Much good work in the early days of small-group research was done with no more ado.

A little later, as studies accumulated, difficulties were bound to arise because it turned out to be impossible to compare findings gained by means of one observation-technique with findings from another. Two observers trained in different ways would notice and name very different events and might have difficulty not only in agreeing about the significance of the events which took place, but indeed about whether they occurred at all. Then again, some of the schedules studied a small area in great detail while others surveyed broad ranges, but the findings from the former could not be conveniently fitted into the latter.

The cause of these difficulties lay in a mistaken idea of the nature of theory (as well as in the contemporary paucity of material). It is not possible to start with an observation-schedule and then build a theory on it. In practice, the design of a schedule grows out of a conscious or unconscious notion that some events are important and worth recording while others can be safely ignored. For one cannot write down everything that happens and it would not be a help if one could. From the total behaviour of the group each research-worker *abstracts* those events in which he is interested. In this way, records are abstractions from 'what really happened'. Moreover, in such selection *classes* of events are singled out for special attention. That is, a conscious or unconscious theoretical decision is made as to which events can be classified under the same heading because they are similar, or under separate headings because they are different. This means that the categories used by one worker may overlap, but in an undefined way, with the categories used by another. Neither need be conscious of the fact that he has a theory: each may seem to himself to be doing what is obviously required.

It may not be out of place to say here that lay people, as much as research-workers, are inconvenienced in this way. They also have a 'recording apparatus' by means of which they select sets of events as outstanding, according to some implicit theory in their mind. The main difference is that, being un-trained, they are even less likely to be aware of it, and therefore more likely to muddle themselves, other things being equal.

Clearly, then, an observation-schedule represents a kind of primitive theory. The events recorded by its means are sub-sequently correlated and a more elaborate theory is developed to account for their occurrence in some circumstances and their absence elsewhere. In the early days, bits of theory and the concepts in which they were clothed, and the observational methods by which they were verified, could be very different from one another. But as more careful theories come into being, better schedules can be formulated to take the new findings into account, and small-group studies have developed with really gratifying speed. Indeed, they have developed to such an extent that general theories of group behaviour are now possible.

A general theory differs from other theories in that it forms a framework for a number of theories each dealing with a particular aspect of group-life. A general theory assumes that behaviour in groups makes sense as a whole, and fits all the partial explanations into one another. In accordance with what has already been said, it should be possible to match a general theory with a general observation-schedule.

Once a general theory is possible, it is economical and pleasing to use it. If everyone uses it, one does not have to keep translating back and forth between words and methods preferred by individuals: they will all use the same framework. When such a general language is established, studies of adjacent areas throw light upon each other, and fruitful new hypotheses are more easily perceived. More studies will provide incidental confirmation of each other. Areas in which more research is needed, because only the broad outlines of events can be guessed at, will be more clearly visible.

This is not to say that everybody will use the whole of the theoretical equipment available. Each experimental worker will confine himself to the area in which he is interested, refining, comparing, connecting. But he will do so within the general framework: he will know where he stands in relation to the rest of the field. These considerations bring us to the final example of this chapter.

3 The theorist working with groups: interaction process analysis

Bales' 'interaction process analysis' was designed primarily in order to satisfy the growing needs for a good observation technique. In addition, it is solidly based on theoretical considerations. It is indeed a remarkable achievement: the most elaborate from the point of view of theory and the simplest from the point of view of analysis.

Let us first look at it simply as an observation-schedule. Each contribution to the discussion is noted in terms of one or more of the categories listed below, together with a note on who contributed, and whether it was directed at a specific other member or at the group as a whole.

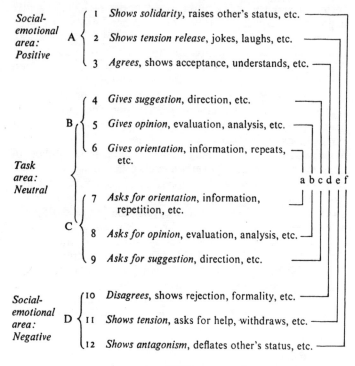

Social-emotional area: Positive   A

1   *Shows solidarity*, raises other's status, etc.

2   *Shows tension release*, jokes, laughs, etc.

3   *Agrees*, shows acceptance, understands, etc.

Task area: Neutral

B

4   *Gives suggestion*, direction, etc.

5   *Gives opinion*, evaluation, analysis, etc.

6   *Gives orientation*, information, repeats, etc.

C

7   *Asks for orientation*, information, repetition, etc.

8   *Asks for opinion*, evaluation, analysis, etc.

9   *Asks for suggestion*, direction, etc.

Social-emotional area: Negative   D

10   *Disagrees*, shows rejection, formality, etc.

11   *Shows tension*, asks for help, withdraws, etc.

12   *Shows antagonism*, deflates other's status, etc.

a b c d e f

KEY

A   Positive reactions

B   Attempted answers

C   Questions

D   Negative reactions

a   Problems of communication

b   Problems of evaluation

c   Problems of control

d   Problems of decision

e   Problems of tension-reduction

f   Problems of reintegration

Particularly to be noted is the interlocking nature of the categories. This feature distinguishes it from the schedules previously discussed and is due to a rigorously theoretical analysis of group events.

Now let us consider the theoretical framework into which it fits. Bales distinguishes first of all between those actions which bring nearer the solution of a group's problems (these he calls contributions in the task-area) and those actions which do not help towards the solution of a common problem (these he calls contributions in the social-emotional area, and we shall later call them 'expressive' contributions).

Task-related contributions take the form of questions or attempted answers, and these in turn involve three consecutive problems which arise in the course of decision-making: communication, evaluation, and control:

Task area

	Questions	Attempted answers
(a) Problem of communication	(asking for or giving orientation, information, repetition, clarification, confirmation, etc.)	
(b) Problem of evaluation	(asking for or giving opinion, evaluation, analysis, expressing feeling, wish, etc.)	
(c) Problem of control	(asking for or giving suggestion, direction, possible ways of action, etc.)	

These three problems are arranged so that the last two nest in their logical predecessors. In other words, if a task is to be performed, this has first to be communicated, then its importance has to be evaluated, and then suggestions for a solution have to be made. This is an extremely important point: there is a logical time-sequence in the decision-making process, and it is convenient for an observation-schedule to take this sequence into account.

Contributions in the social-emotional area can be classified according to the same pattern:

Social-emotional area

	Positive reactions	Negative reactions
(d) Problem of decision	(agrees, shows passive acceptance, understands, concurs, complies, etc.)	(disagrees, shows passive rejection, formality, withholds help, etc.)
(e) Problem of tension-reduction	(shows tension-release, jokes, laughs, shows satisfaction, etc.)	(shows tension, asks for help, withdraws out of field, etc.)
(f) Problem of reintegration	(shows solidarity, raises other's status, gives help, reward, etc.)	(shows antagonism, deflates other's status, defends or asserts self, etc.)

These three are also to be thought of as belonging to the logical time-sequence of decision-making. When agreement is reached, the tension relaxes and people are free to show their pleasure in each other's company.

Finally, we may see how the scheme can help experimental and practical workers with groups. For this, larger categories like 'leadership', 'differences of opinion', and 'difficulty of the task' are required. Bales does this by using his records to construct compound indices. Take, for instance, 'differences of opinion'. He calls this 'difficulty of evaluation' and defines it as the number of negative contributions to the problem of evaluation in proportion to the total number of contributions in this category:

$$\frac{8}{8+5}$$

In the same way, type of leadership is identifiable from his 'index of directiveness of control':

$$\frac{4}{4+6} + \frac{5}{5+6}$$

There are a number of ingenious constructions of this kind, but we need not go into them all here.

Nevertheless, the scheme is open to criticism on several

grounds. The flaws begin to appear when one tries to use it for observing group-interaction: the categories look tidier than they in fact are. The contents are less easily distinguished than the labels on the packet suggest. Therefore, although much in later chapters is inspired by Bales—and the distinction between task-related and social-emotional or expressive interaction is fundamental—alternative formulations will be frequently suggested. In the final chapter, the outcome of all these modifications and considerations will be presented.

BIBLIOGRAPHY

Observation-schedules

Wilson G. and Ryland G., *Social Group Work Practice* (Houghton Mifflin, Boston, 1949), pp. 178 ff.

Zander A., 'The WP Club: an objective case-study of a group', *Human Relations* I (1948).

Heyns R. and Lippit R., 'Systematic Observation Techniques', Lindzey (ed.), *Handbook of Social Psychology* (Addison-Wesley, Cambridge, Mass., 1954).

Bales R. F., *Interaction Process Analysis* (Addison-Wesley, Cambridge, Mass., 1951).

General theory in the study of small groups

Homans G., *The Human Group* (Harcourt Brace, New York, 1950).

Bales R. F., *Interaction Process Analysis* (Addison-Wesley, Cambridge, Mass., 1951).

Parsons T., Bales R. F., and Shils E., *Working Papers in the Theory of Action* (Free Press, Illinois, 1953).

Stogdill R. M., *Individual Behaviour and Group Achievement* (Oxford U.P., 1959).

Thibaut J. W. and Kelley H. H., *The Social Psychology of Groups* (Wiley, New York; Chapman and Hall, London, 1959).

Theory and observation in small groups

Cartwright D. and Zander A. (ed.), *Group Dynamics* (Row, Peterson, New York, 1956), ch. 1.

Homans G., *The Human Group* (Harcourt Brace, New York, 1950), ch. 1.

3

TASK-RELATED BEHAVIOUR AND THE DECISION-MAKING SEQUENCE

The task of a decision-making group is to reach unanimous agreement on a course of action. Such agreement depends on a unique combination of the values of the members and the facts at their disposal. The decision-making sequence therefore requires exchanges of information and of views before agreement can be reached. All other contributions to the discussion are irrelevant to the problem under consideration and must be treated as expressive of personal idiosyncrasies.

WHY do people meet for discussion in groups? It is, of course, an enjoyable activity: hearing others give their point of view stimulates our ideas. But, also, we want to make up our mind and so come to a conclusion. This conclusion is likely—more than is perhaps realized at first—to be a social matter. An exchange of ideas is felt to be incomplete if it does not lead to harmony, to a shared conclusion. A man does not only want to make up his mind; he wants to be of one mind with others.

Generally speaking, then, it is the function of a discussion group to combine ideas into a coherent whole: a plan or a decision acceptable to all members. The present book is no more than a development of this definition. Accordingly, it is appropriate first of all to examine the nature of the ideas that are to be exchanged. How are they to be recognized and classified?

In logic, ideas are said to have two aspects: a fact aspect and a value aspect. Some ideas concern easily verifiable matters of fact: for example, that Jones no longer lives in the city, or that the bus leaves the station at 10.15. The exchange of ideas is, then, sometimes an exchange of items of fact. In a group, this happens during the stage of information-exchange. When

30

members of a group exchange information, each contributes from his own experience to the group's little pile of common knowledge. By this means, the factual limitations which must be taken into account when making a decision are stated or explored. No amount of discussion can alter facts. Facts are impersonal.

On the other hand, some ideas concern judgments of value or statements of preference: for example, that one ought not to spend public money carelessly, or that all the furniture in a room should be contemporary. There is no way of verifying these ideas; indeed the notion of verification is inapplicable to them; one can only hope to persuade others of their attractiveness or moral grandeur (or indicate, as we shall see in later chapters, that one has no time for people who do not see things in the same way). These ideas are often more deeply felt, and more tenaciously held, than are mere facts. Values and preferences are personal. The expression of values and preferences states or explores the social and emotional limits which members of the group wish to take into account when making a decision. Unless these values and preferences are taken into account, members will not wish to be associated with the group, or with a particular decision.

This division of ideas into matters of fact and judgments of value is a commonplace in logic. But it is not a commonplace in people's minds, or in their behaviour. First of all, people do not normally state, in so many words, the values by which they live, and they are often too polite or too diffident to express their preferences directly. Indeed, they are sometimes unaware of their own values and preferences. They take them for granted. Secondly, as is to be expected—language itself being a social construct—people in conversation do not draw a line between facts and values. Subjectively all ideas feel like knowledge. For their possessor they are self-evident and self-validating, so that decisions are built into the very way in which the problem is stated.

When people talk to each other, therefore, they tend to convey an amalgam of facts and values in the same sentence, and, as a rule, neither the speaker nor his listener pauses to make the distinction. If they were asked what they were doing, they would say that they were exchanging views. 'Views' are sentences in which facts and values are presented in a ready-made combination. When, for instance, a man says that the railways could be run more economically, he is saying something about the value of economy *and* something about the way the railways are run at present. Of course, for the formation of a plan, facts and values have to be combined. But often, as in this example, the combination is made prematurely: neither the speaker nor his hearer has had the opportunity of examining the truth of the given facts or his preference for the values involved, before consciously fitting them into an acceptable whole.

Between them, facts and values determine the course of decision-making. This course is now to be examined, with the aid of an example.

A model of a task-related interaction-sequence

1. How shall we arrange the furniture in this room?
2. What furniture is there?
3. There is a desk, a tall bookcase, and a small cupboard.
4. We should avoid putting the desk in a draught.
5. Yes.
6. That means we can't put it by the window.
7. Now where shall we put that bookcase?
8. The only place where it will fit is by the door.
9. It will also fit by the radiator.
10. Have you measured it?
11. Yes.
12. Let's put it by the door then.
13. O.K.
14. And the desk by the radiator.
15. Oh no.

This little dialogue is bound to sound stilted. It is designed to show the categories of interaction at their simplest, and all difficulties have been avoided. The conversation turns on one problem: how to dispose the furniture in a room. All contributions are relevant to the solution of this problem—that is one reason why the whole thing sounds stilted.

It will be noted that agreement on the nature of the problem has been reached before the sequence opens.

Before any problem can be solved, the facts need to be established. Accordingly, sequence 1–15 includes requests for *information*: 'What furniture is there?' and items of information: 'There is a desk, a bookcase, and a cupboard'. The information may be correct, insufficient or incorrect. That the desk would be in the draught by the window is a piece of information that goes unchallenged; we must assume that it is considered adequate and correct. The information that the bookcase will only fit by the door, on the other hand, is challenged. When a member considers an item of information inadequate, he may do three things. He may contradict, as in contribution 9: 'It will also fit by the radiator' and this is a further item of information to be taken into account by the group. Or he may ask for further information to be given on the matter, as in contributions 10 and 11: 'Have you measured it?', 'Yes'. Or he may himself explore the point further and provide the additional information he considers necessary, as in contribution 6: 'That means we can't put it by the window'.

However, information by itself can only solve the simplest problems. Given the dimensions of the furniture and of the room, many different arrangements are still possible. The final outcome will depend on members' preferences. Therefore *views* have to be expressed before agreement can be reached. 'We should avoid putting the desk in a draught' is a characteristic expression of a view. Technically and pompously, we could say that draught-avoidance is the value-element, and the disposition of door, window, and desk the fact-element.

Views are sometimes expressed as *explicit proposals*, as in 'Let's put it by the door then'. We shall see later that it is sometimes convenient to keep a separate account of explicit proposals. All proposals are classifiable as views, being simply combinations of facts and values of a special kind. They are recommendations that facts and values be combined *in a particular way*. Thus 'We should avoid putting the desk in a draught' implies a proposal that draught-avoidance shall be the preference governing the disposition of the desk. 'Let's put it by the door' is an explicit version of this proposal.

In the same way that information-giving has its converse in asking for information, so giving views has its converse in asking for views. Requests for information are often, but not always, easily recognized. They may be confused with requests for views, into which they tend to merge, as in 'Can I ring you tomorrow?' or 'Would you like a biscuit?' Requests for information should only be scored as such when they are unmistakably and exclusively factual, without overtones of any kind. As soon as values enter, or even if it looks as though values might enter, the requests are disqualified from being scored as factual, for the logical difference between facts and preferences, or between information-exchange and disputes over values, is so important that the observer must keep it in mind, even if the group members are a little muddled about it.

Views may meet with approval and agreement, or they may not. Oddly enough, 'yes' and 'no' are sometimes difficult to classify. They are to be scored as information when no evaluative element is present, i.e. when they are reactions to requests for information, as in 'Have you measured it?', 'Yes'. Any other contribution has an evaluative element in it, and 'yes' and 'no' would be evaluative reactions, therefore to be scored as *agreement or disagreement*, as in 'We should avoid putting the desk in a draught', 'Yes', and 'And the desk by the radiator', 'Oh no'.

When the members agree, the decision-making sequence comes to an end, since the purpose of the discussion—'the combination of facts and values into a coherent whole, acceptable to all members'—has been achieved. If a member disagrees, this indicates that some ideas have been left out of the proposed combination, which is thereby rendered unacceptable to someone. These ideas will have to be made explicit, and new combinations brought forward for acceptance by the group.

Ideally, the course of the decision-making process therefore runs as follows:

> previous decision as to priority of problems
> exchange of information
> exchange of views (sometimes an explicit proposal)
> agreement *or*
> disagreement with further exchange of information and
>   views
> agreement *or*
> disagreement with further exchange . . . , etc.

Conversation 1–15 can be expanded in the following way
to make clear what categories of interaction are involved:

1.	*Would someone give his views* about the way to arrange the furniture in this room?	vi—
2.	*Please tell me* what furniture there is.	inf—
3.	*The fact is* that there is a desk, a tall bookcase, and a small cupboard.	inf+
4.	*In my view* we should avoid putting the desk in a draught.	vi+
5.	*I agree.*	agr+
6.	*An additional relevant fact* is that we can't put it by the window.	inf+
7.	*Would someone give his views* about the place of the bookcase?	vi—
8.	*The fact is* that it will only fit by the door.	inf+
9.	*The fact is* that it will also fit by the radiator	inf+
10.	*Please tell me* if you have measured it.	inf—
11.	*The fact is* that I have.	inf+
12.	*In my view* it should stand by the door.	vi+
13.	*I agree.*	agr+
14.	*In my view* the desk could stand by the radiator.	vi+
15.	*I disagree.*	agr—

The analysis of that aspect of interaction which enables
the group to be business-like has now been completed.

With the next conversation a quite new type of behaviour

is introduced and accordingly also a new category for analysis. As soon as feelings are allowed to enter into a conversation the dialogue begins to sound really natural, more like the kind of thing we are used to.

A model of a task-related interaction-sequence, with self-expressive interruptions

16. The only problem left now is where to put the chairs.
17. You've got four altogether.
18. That's right.
19. Let's leave it till tomorrow.
20. I shan't be here tomorrow and it must be tidy before the weekend.
21. All right then. I daresay the chairs could stand over there.
22. Do you want to concentrate them like that?
23. No, but I don't see how else to do it.
24. If the chairs were by the wall, they would be out of the way.
25. I don't like the way it would make the room look narrow.
26. That can't be helped.
27. I'm fed up. Let's go to the pictures.
28. You're just a nuisance.
29. Come on, we're doing fine. After this we'll be finished.
30. I suggest one chair by the desk, two by the window, and one just here.
31. I don't mind that.
32. I don't think I like it like that. Goodness, you should see the fog!

The new type of interaction, found in contributions 27, 28, 29, and 32, is purely expressive, and must be carefully distinguished from task-related interaction. The distinction does not lie in the depth or beauty of feeling expressed, but in the fact that it is strictly irrelevant to the problem-solving sequence. This is a trap for the unwary, for some views sound expressive, and some self-expressive statements sound like views. For instance, 'It must be tidy before the weekend' and 'I don't like the way it would make the room look narrow' are statements of personal feeling, but because they are relevant to the decision facing the group, they are classified as views.

In contrast, we have 'I'm fed up', 'Let's go to the pictures', and 'You should see the fog!' These statements are irrelevant to the solution of the problem: they do not bring a decision nearer. More concretely, they do not add information about the problem of where the chairs are to be put, they do not ask for views thereon, they do not propose a course of action as far as the disposal of the furniture is concerned, nor do they express agreement or disagreement with a proposal to put the chairs in a certain position.

The care to be taken in analysing the interaction-process is demonstrated by contributions 17 and 18: 'You've got four [chairs] altogether', 'That's right'. The first of these is obviously information-giving. 'That's right' is not informative, it is not a view, and it is not agreement, because it does not follow a view or a proposal. It does not help the task on: it is therefore irrelevant, expressive of friendliness towards the previous speaker.

Like task-related interaction, expressive interaction has a positive and a negative side. Positive we shall call those contributions which are irrelevant, but friendly, morale-building, and obviously cohesive in effect. Negative are those contributions which are irrelevant, morale-destroying and, on the face of it, disruptive. There are two kinds of negative self-expression: hostility and withdrawal. Withdrawal refers to the flight of a member from the group or the task, his dissociation and retreat. To illustrate:

'I'm fed up'	expresses hostility (to task)
'Let's go to the pictures'	expresses withdrawal (from task)
'You're just a nuisance'	expresses hostility (to a member)
'We're doing fine'	expresses friendliness (to task and group)
'You should see the fog'	expresses withdrawal (from task)

The conversation-sequence now under examination also sounds more natural because, as the reader will recognize upon reflection, two decisions are being reached in it, not just one. The main decision concerns the disposal of the furniture. The minor task is set, discussed and successfully terminated in contributions 19–21. Here a proposal is made to postpone the main task of the group to another day, whereupon information is given and a view expressed which goes against the acceptance of that proposal. 'All right then' in 21 is agreement with the view in 20 that tidiness before the weekend is a value which must be taken into consideration. 'Let's leave it till tomorrow' is thus irrelevant to the main problem and expressive of withdrawal, and at the same time a proposal that a different problem be considered. The division of interaction-sequences into episodes, which are demarcated by proposals to change from one task to another, is normal whenever people talk for any length of time. How this works out in practice will become clearer in chapter 11.

Lastly, the conversation sounds more natural because the members are leaving things unsaid, implying a variety of meanings in their contributions. Accordingly, these contributions will have to be scored under more than one heading. Where agreement or disagreement is implied this may be indicated in brackets. The total interaction-schedule now follows:

Task-related, factual only	asks for information	inf—
	gives information	inf+
Task-related, combining facts and values	asks for views	vi—
	gives views	vi+
	makes explicit proposal (optional category)	pro+
	disagrees	agr—
	agrees	agr+
Task-irrelevant, expressive, evaluative only	expresses hostility	expr—h
	expresses withdrawal	expr—w
	expresses friendliness	expr+f

Expanded, conversation 16–32 reads thus:

16. *In fact*, there is only one problem left now, where to put the chairs. — inf+

17. *In fact*, there are four chairs. — inf+

18. Irrelevant expression of *friendliness*. — expr+f

19. I *withdraw* from that problem and propose a new one more important *in my view*. — expr−w, vi+

20. I *imply disagreement* with the new proposal. *The fact is* that I shan't be here tomorrow and *in my view* it should be tidy before the weekend. — agr− (impl), inf+, vi+

21. *I agree.* I give *a view* about the place for the chairs. — agr+, vi+

22. *Will you say some more* on this subject? — vi−

23. *The fact* is that I don't want to put them there, but the *fact is*, there is nowhere else to put them. — inf+, inf+

24. *The fact* is that they could stand by the wall, and *in my view* it is important to have them out of the way. — inf+, vi+

25. I *imply disagreement* with the proposal implied in the previous view. *In my view* this would make the room look narrow. — agr− (impl), vi+

26. *The fact is* that can't be helped. *I imply disagreement* with the proposal implied in the previous view. — inf+, agr− (impl)

27. *I dislike* the situation and *withdraw* from it. I propose a new activity, *in my view* more important. — expr−h, expr−w, vi+

28. *Irrelevant* expression of *hostility*. — expr−h

29. *Irrelevant* expression of *friendliness. The fact* is that the task is nearly finished. — expr+f, inf+

30. *In my view* we should put one chair by the desk, and two by the window. — vi+

31. *I agree.* — agr+

32. *In my view* that is not a good proposal.   vi+
    I imply disagreement and *withdraw* from   agr— (impl)
    the problem.   expr—w

4

TASK-RELATED BEHAVIOUR AND THE
FUNCTIONS OF MEMBERS

In all task-related groups the following useful functions have to be performed: giving information, asking for contributions from other members, making proposals, and maintaining morale. The roles corresponding to these functions are respectively: the expert, the facilitator, the co-ordinator, and the morale-builder.

AT FIRST sight the previous chapter may have seemed unduly strict and 'scientific'; it is hoped that this will not have discouraged the reader. There is only one way of participating in the making of decisions while remaining at the same time aware of what is going on in the group at other levels; and that is: to train one's perceptions to do their work subconsciously. For that purpose it is necessary to have the basic categories into which conversation falls, fixed firmly in the mind. When this has been achieved, one can relax. It is like learning the multiplication tables in childhood, so that later one may perform simple calculations without having to think about them. Just as to an adult 7×8 *means* 56, without an intervening thought-process, so, it is hoped, the reader will learn to register without an effort of the attention the meaning of what is being said and done in a group. For that purpose, much practice and discussion at what may appear an elementary level is necessary.

This chapter is concerned with the way in which the members of the group use the categories of interaction: information, views, and agreement. The first section is simple and schematic, drawing directly on the previous chapter, in which the task-structure was seen as composed of interacting categories, to build up a conception of a group-structure of interacting members. The second section deals more discursively with some types of members commonly found in groups, for different people contribute in different and characteristic ways to a discussion.

To develop the argument, sequence 16–32 is reproduced below, with the interaction-categories unchanged, but the contributions imputed to four members of a group.

The structure of an informal decision-making group

Alan: The only problem left now is where to put the chairs. — inf+

Don: You've got four altogether. — inf+

Brian: That's right. — expr+f

Don: Let's leave it till tomorrow. — vi+, expr—w

Alan: I shan't be here tomorrow and it must be tidy before the weekend. — agr— (impl) inf+, vi+

Charles: All right then. I daresay the chairs could stand over there. — agr+, vi+

Brian: Do we want to concentrate them like that? — vi—

Charles: No, but I don't see how else to do it. — inf+, inf+

Alan: If the chairs were by the wall, they would be out of the way. — vi+, inf+

Brian: I don't like the way it would make the room look narrow. — agr— (impl) vi+

Alan: That can't be helped. — agr— (impl) inf+

Don: I'm fed up. Let's go to the pictures. — vi+, expr—h expr—w

Charles: You're just a nuisance. — expr—h

Brian: Come on, we're doing fine. After this we'll be finished. — expr+f inf+

Charles: I suggest one chair by the desk, two by the window and one just here. — vi+

Brian: I wouldn't mind that. — agr+

Don: I don't think I like it like that. Goodness, you should see the fog outside! — agr—(impl) vi+, expr—w

One should not, of course, generalize from so short a sequence, which may be quite uncharacteristic of the people involved in it, but this one has been specifically constructed to clarify some important points. By listening carefully, one gets the feeling that Alan is something of a leader, that Brian is a pleasant sort of person, that Charles wants to get on with the job, and that Don is correctly described as a nuisance. An analysis of their contributions bears this out.

Who gives information? Who gives views? Who encourages others to contribute? Who agrees or disagrees? Who expresses friendliness, hostility, or a desire to get away? In tabular form:

inf+	AAAA	B	CC D	inf—		
vi+	AA	B	CC DDD	vi—		B
agr+		B	C	agr—	AA B	D
expr+f		BB		expr—h		C D
				expr—w		DDD

We see that Alan gives far more information than anyone else. Twice in this short sequence he disagrees. He is the only member not to engage in expressive behaviour of any kind. Brian's pleasant character shows itself in that he is the only one to ask someone else for his views, and in that he twice expresses friendliness. He is less task-related than the others, and more interested than they are in keeping things going well. Charles is, like Alan, a rather task-related member, but more in terms of views than of facts. Don interacts mainly in the expressive, value-loaded range. Two of his views are proposals to withdraw from the task.

But this is not a complete picture. One must know not only how members contribute to the group, but also how their contributions are received. Whose views receive support? Whose requests for information are given consideration? At whom is friendliness or hostility directed? This becomes clearer with the construction of an *interaction-matrix*, often called, more informally, a *who-to-whom table*.

Interaction-matrix

	to A	to B	to C	to D	to Group
from A		agr− (impl) inf+		agr− (impl) inf+, vi+	inf+, inf+ inf+, vi+
from B	agr− (impl) vi+		vi− agr+	expr+f	expr+f inf+
from C	agr+	inf+, inf+		expr−h	vi+, vi+
from D		agr− (impl)			inf+, vi+ expr−w, vi+ expr−w, expr−h expr−w

The picture now becomes more distinct. Although Alan gives a lot of information, he is never directly asked for it. When Alan disagrees, he adds his views or information. Brian and Charles express their feelings directly to the people concerned, whereas Don tends to air his to the group in general. Brian, an attractive member, is the direct recipient of contributions more often than the others. The others tend to receive either contributions in the agreement-category or expressions of feelings.

One other type of analysis is sometimes used. A rough impression can often be gained of where the centre of a member's interests lies, whether in himself or in other members of the group or in those outside, and of the extent to which he feels identified with the group or out of it, simply by counting how often he says 'I' (or me), 'we' (or us), you, he, they, etc. A fine example of this is given by Arthur Koestler in *Darkness at Noon*:

'Why actually,' [said Rubashov,] 'do you people intend to have me shot?' Ivanov let a few seconds go by ... 'Listen, Rubashov,' he said finally. 'There is one thing I would like to point out to you. You have now repeatedly said "you" —meaning State and Party, as opposed to "I"—that is, Nicholas Salmanovitch Rubashov. For the public, one needs, of course, a trial and legal justification. For us, what I have just said should be enough.'

	I	we	you	impersonal
Alan	1			4
Brian	2	3		1
Charles	3		1	1
Don	3	2	2	

Alan, the factually minded, tends to use the impersonal form of statement, not bringing either himself or other members of the group into the picture as persons. Brian, the warmly expressive, identified with the group, talks in terms of 'we'. Charles, more task-related, is also less group-centred.

Don forms a contrast to Alan, being very personal in his contributions.

Here is a group with a different kind of task.

The structure of a formal decision-making group

Robinson: The next case is Mr Johnson. He has been accepted at the University and is applying for a maintenance-grant. What information have we about him?	inf+ inf+ inf—
Secretary: (gives information)	inf+
Taylor: His father is a well-to-do doctor?	vi—
Underhill: I disagree with that. It should make no difference to us. There are four other children to be educated.	agr— (value: parental responsibility) vi+ (same value) inf+
Taylor: I disapprove of the modern tendency to make local authorities pay for every circumstance of life.	agr— (value: parental responsibility) vi+ (same value)
Robinson: What is his school record?	inf—
Secretary: (gives information)	inf+
Robinson: This young man has a very good school record indeed.	vi+ (value: importance of good past)
Williams: We should give him a chance at the University without financial worries.	vi+ (value: independence)
Underhill: How should we assess the amount of the grant?	vi—
Taylor: Should we consider the fact that he will be staying at home during the vacation?	vi—
Williams: What is our present policy as regards vacation work to earn money?	inf—
Robinson: There are a number of considerations to be taken into account.	inf+

Taylor: I agree that it would be unjust to expect a man to give up his studies during the vacation in order to support himself. — vi+ (value: independence)

Williams: Taking all things into consideration he should clearly get a grant. I should say that the grant should be the same as that given in the previous case. — vi+ vi+

Robinson: Are the members of the committee agreed? — inf—

Omnes: Yes. — agr+

The interaction process is distributed between the members in the following way:

inf+	RRR	SS		U		inf—	RRR			W
vi+	R		TT	U	WW	vi—	.	TT	U	
agr+	(all in final contribution)					agr—		T	U	

Robinson confines himself to giving and seeking information. It is not hard to imagine him as the chairman of a rather 'difficult' committee. A chairman does not usually talk quite as much as this, at least according to the conventions, but his guidance seems unobtrusive. On the one occasion that he departs from information-exchange to give his own view, the fact-element (i.e. the marks obtained) is more important than the value-element (i.e. a good school-record as a qualification for a grant).

The secretary does what good secretaries do, and confines himself to giving information.

Taylor is a typical view-giver. Nowhere does he confine himself to the facts without putting them in the context of his own values and preferences. The value-element in his contributions is strong.

Underhill contributes in all categories.

Williams makes the only proposal that is made explicitly, and it is accepted. (He makes it twice.) It is to be noted that Williams comes into the discussion at a relatively late stage. This is often a characteristic of those who specialize in proposals, since it allows all available ideas to be aired before they combine them into an acceptable proposal.

	to R	to S	to T	to U	to W	to Group
from R	inf— inf—				inf+	inf+, inf+ vi+, inf—
from S						inf+, inf+
from T			agr— vi+			vi—, vi— vi+
from U			agr— vi+ inf+			vi—
from W						vi+, vi— vi+, vi+

The interaction-matrix brings out an incompatibility of views between Underhill and Taylor, but generally is most notable for its confirmation of the business-like attitude of this committee. The chairman addresses the secretary twice for information, and Williams' importance is confirmed in that the chairman addresses him personally. Apart from this, and the exception of Underhill and Taylor as noted above, all members address themselves to the group as a whole. They do not engage in private discussion. The secretary confines himself to giving information when asked for it. He does not speak on his own account.

The I-we-you chart, to which has been added a category 'others' to allow us to gauge the extent to which Mr Johnson and his circumstances are concretely referred to, shows the same business-like and humane attitude.

	I	we	you	others	impersonal
Robinson ..		1		5	2
Taylor ..	2	1		3	
Underhill ..	1	2			1
Williams ..	1	2		2	

This table shows once again that the chairman is more impersonal than the others, never refers to himself, and refers frequently to those outside the group, who form, after all, the subject-matter of this committee. Taylor, a rather expressive view-giver, refers somewhat more often to himself. The absence of private discussion is brought out by the absence of the use of the second person singular.

Starting with an analysis of the interaction-categories essential to the successful (i.e. sensible and agreed) performance of a task, we have now come to the point where we are able to see the members of the group as the pegs on which the interaction-pattern of the group is hung—all the aspects necessary for task-performance have to be distributed among the members of the group.

When the differences between members' contributions to the performance of a task are analysed, it becomes apparent that each member tends to contribute in a unique way to what happens in the group. Each member has a somewhat different function, or, it is often said, 'plays a different role'.

A man plays a role when he performs a particular function, which is usually closely circumscribed by the expectations of others with whom he interacts in performing that function. A man will, in this sense, play the role of father, i.e. perform the function of a father, when he tells his son to go to school; he will play the role of foreman, i.e. perform his function as foreman, when he tells a worker to start on a new piece of work; he plays the role of churchwarden, i.e. performs his function of churchwarden, when he hands round the collection-plate in church. The son, the workman, the congregation, recognize his role and respond in accordance with their town.

Another way of saying this, is that a man's role is his response whenever he finds himself in certain socially defined situations. He is not, normally or necessarily, conscious of defining his own role, although an observer can often perceive that he plays the same role from meeting to meeting. Indeed, he cannot absolutely determine his own role, because it is affected by the behaviour of others in the group. Since this is true for each member of the group in his relation to others, it is permissible to speak of the role-structure of the group.

Not all that can be said about role-structure can be drawn from the two sample-sequences used in this chapter. But with their help, and with the help of the theory previously outlined, it is possible to make a start on a subject which will become very important in later chapters. We therefore end this chapter with a quick look at that aspect of role-behaviour which concerns a man's initiation of interaction. Other aspects, which take into account the reception of interaction, will be dealt with in chapters 8 and 9.

First, then, it is clear that some people may be characteristically information-givers. They play the role of *experts.* Other members depend on them for facts. A man may be an expert in a field of study, or he may have special experience of the problem, or he may have contacts outside the group through which he gains special insight; in any case, the others lean on him for his expert knowledge. Often there is more than one expert in the group: each has his own expertise.

Another member of the group, though not necessarily himself highly informed, may be good at knowing what contributions are lacking. In accordance with our theory, this might take two forms. His gifts might be restricted to the factual side of the decision-making process. That is, it may be that he recognizes easily what information might be relevant, though he himself does not possess it. By asking for such information he may enable another member, who happens to know those facts but is slower at seeing their relevance, to make his contribution; or he may get the group to invite an outside expert for the purpose. In this way he allows more information to be pooled than would otherwise have been the case. Or his gifts might lie more generally in encouraging other members to contribute to the discussion, in seeing that they are all enabled to give their viewpoint. For it is never to be supposed that quieter members are less important or less knowledgeable. Since such a member facilitates the exchange of information and of views, he would be called the *facilitator.*

Chapter 10 is devoted to an analysis of the techniques he has at his disposal.

· The combination of facts and values into an acceptable whole requires the presence in the group of what may be called organizational experts or *co-ordinators*. Such members do not necessarily take part in putting forward relevant facts, and they do not necessarily have an axe of their own to grind. Their talent lies in seeing how the views of different members may be reconciled and what formulation will take into account both the available facts and the wishes of the group. Such people will be particularly active in making explicit proposals. Williams was such a one.

The role of members who do not contribute their views in the form of explicit proposals depends almost entirely on other members' reactions to their views. A discussion of this aspect is postponed until chapter 8.

Lastly, there are members who specialize in expressive contributions, irrelevant to the task. These may be simply a nuisance, like the quarrelsome and the lackadaisical who tend to disrupt the group. Others may be useful in relation to the group, even when useless to the task as strictly defined. These may be *morale-builders*, like Brian, bringing warmth to the group by their encouraging, though irrelevant, remarks. Their function is discussed in more detail in chapter 9.

BIBLIOGRAPHY

Benne K. and Sheats W., 'Functional roles of group-members', *J. Social Issues* IV, 1948.

Reissman L., 'Study of role-conceptions in bureaucracy', *Social Forces* XXVI (1949).

Neiman L. J. and Hughes J. W., 'The concept of role', *Social Forces* XXVIII (1951).

Bales R. F., *Interaction Process Analysis*, op. cit., ch. 5.

Bales R. F., Couch A. S., and Borgatta E. F., 'The consistency of subject-behaviour and the reliability of scoring in interaction process analysis', Hare, Borgatta and Bales (ed.), *Small Groups* (Knopf, New York, 1952–5), ch. 6.

Bates F. L., 'Position, role and status', *Social Forces* XXXIII (1956). 'A conceptual analysis of group structure', *Social Forces* XXXIV (1957).

Gross N., Martin W. S., and McEachern A. W., *Explorations in Role Analysis* (Wiley, New York, 1958).

Levinson D. J., 'Role, Personality and Social Structure', *J. Abnormal and Social Psych.* LVIII (1958).

5

THE PSYCHOLOGICAL SIGNIFICANCE
OF SELF-EXPRESSION AND
GROUP-MEMBERSHIP

Self-expression and the sympathetic response of others give the individual an assurance of his own worth. The family creates these needs, which are later satisfied in other groups. The satisfaction of these needs depends on conformity with the outlook of the group: whether self-expression is approved depends on the extent to which the group approves of the self expressed. The group exercises control over its members: an individual who lacks adequate social contacts tends to deviate in ways which cause him to be rejected. The desire to belong may lead a man to change his outlook. Increased security of group-membership permits an increased independence of outlook.

THE preliminary treatment of task-related aspects of inter-action is now over and our present concern is task-irrelevant expressive behaviour. This will be considered in the current chapter in terms of its function for the individual. In chapter 6 expressive interaction will be considered from the point of view of the function it plays in the group.

Expressive interaction springs from the feelings of members as individual people: their values, their goals, their motives, their whole personality, of which the wish to co-operate in the performance of some group's task is only one manifestation: it is their *self*-expression. We must therefore consider some of the roots of this need for self-expression in order to answer such questions as: Why does the individual need the group? What does the group do for the individual? Why does a member engage in self-expressive behaviour when the co-operative performance of a task does not require it? Briefly, the answer will be that the individual has learnt to expect from the group an affirmation of his value as an individual, and that self-expressive behaviour—i.e. behaviour that springs from his own feelings rather than from the requirements of the task—elicits this gratifying affirmation.

Three interrelated generalizations epitomize the social significance of group-membership in our culture. The individual needs his group's assurance that he is valued; he gains it by behaving in a manner acceptable to the group; and, when he does this, he gives to others that same assurance of individual worth which he gains from them. We shall consider how individuals come to possess the kind of mind for which these three generalizations are true. Then we shall look at the function of the group in cases where one of the conditions governing this behavioural complex is missing, i.e. where the individual lacks groups which give him this assurance—this we shall call social hunger, or where he cannot exchange gratifying self-expression because his own behaviour is not regarded by others as acceptable—this we shall call social ignorance. In both sections of this chapter we shall anticipate a later discussion in chapter 6 and relate these conditions to the exercise of social control.

The expectation of satisfactions from group-membership derives to a large extent from the primacy of the family in the individual's experience. By being born into a family, he is shaped so as to seek out others for the satisfaction of his needs in many ways. Before he is aware of himself as a self-conscious being, while he is yet entirely dependent on others for the satisfaction of his material wants, he and others already depend on one another for the satisfaction of social and emotional needs. This need for interdependence will remain with him for the rest of his life: he will need to live his life in the context of small groups of others.

It is in the family that he learns that he is a valued person: here what he does and what he says is encouraged and approved. It is this which gives him the conviction that he is valued. He also learns that others are pleased when he inter-acts with them: his expression of himself enhances their individuality and worth. It is this which gives him the con-viction that self-expression on his part is gratifying to others. Within the family, assurances of worth are exchanged between socially and emotionally interdependent persons when each is expressing himself. It is easy for an unsophisticated person to assume that self-expression is mutually gratifying in all groups.

Self-expression in the family is not, of course, regarded as a good without qualification. Rather it is the expression of a certain kind of self—a socialized self—which is approved and rewarded. As the child is socialized, he comes to share the outlook of his family. He learns to laugh at what they think funny, to approve what they commend. He learns to avoid the kinds of self-expression which are not received with gratification and which are therefore less gratifying to him. It is the expression of family-approved ideas which affirms his own worth and that of those to whom he directs himself, and it is the expression of these ideas which strengthens the family as a social group, with a life of its own, to which it is a pleasure and a privilege to belong.

Having briefly indicated some of the childhood origins of the need to live a social life, we may examine the nature of the adult's social and emotional dependence on the group. Following an honourable tradition, we will start with an extreme case. Just as theories of personality-development originated largely from the study of abnormal psychology, so it may be fruitful to consider what happens in a group of maladjusted members. The maladjusted may possess needs so strong that they show through the normal tendency to con-form to prevailing cultural patterns of behaviour. Fundamental psychic mechanisms are not covered over to the same extent by considerations of courtesy, good manners or self-conscious-ness: they therefore show more clearly. In somewhat the same way, the social behaviour of maladjusted persons may allow us to see social mechanisms less easily observed in the normal group. Such groups are available to systematic study because of the growing popularity of group-psychotherapy.

Psychotherapy in groups seems to have begun first of all as a happy historical accident, when there were more patients than the psychiatrist could deal with singly. As recovery was in some cases more rapid, theories were constructed to account for its success.

As is to be expected, one set of theories was mainly concerned with family-relationships. In the therapeutic group (and not infrequently elsewhere) the trained observer can see how parent-child, inter-sex and inter-sib relationships are re-enacted, sometimes at a very primitive level. The recovery of the patient is thought to be due to the curative effect of reliving these experiences in a group where the psychiatrist can interpret and modify their expression.

It is not with this aspect that we are primarily concerned. We are interested in social and emotional aspects of group-behaviour, and a group whose main task is the improvement of these expressive relationships may give us some useful guidance. For this reason those types of group-psychotherapy which are irrelevant to the present purpose, and such considerations as types of illness and types of therapeutic technique, are disregarded. What follows must not be looked on as a review of the scope of group psychotherapeutic practices. But many of the events in the therapeutic group bear a close resemblance to events which happen in the normal friendship-group, and even in the task-performing group. By looking carefully at the therapeutic group we can clarify our ideas on the function of the same events in normal groups, in the life of the ordinary man.

We shall argue that the patient in a therapeutic group suffers, because his self-expression is inappropriate, from two conditions which mutually aggravate each other: social hunger and social ignorance. A man who does not know the proper way to behave, or is unable to behave in conformity with the expectations of others, will express himself 'inappropriately'. If he does so too frequently or too markedly, people will not put up with him. But social ignorance can only be mended with experience or by teaching. If therefore an individual is isolated from social life, he becomes progressively more ignorant, behaves more inappropriately, is again rejected, and loses touch still further because of his ignorance of social realities.

Social ignorance thus creates social hunger. This is a very real hunger, for the individual's assurance of his worth depends on group-membership. The relationship between these must now be examined in detail.

Self-expression and social hunger

In the light of what has been said above, it should not be surprising that a good deal of the conversation one hears in a therapeutic group sounds like perfectly ordinary conversation, which could be heard at any party. Its significance there is the same as its significance anywhere. It is simply pleasant to talk, to say what comes to mind and to hear what others have in their mind. The mutual exchange of self-expressive behaviour, to put it formally, is mutually gratifying because this behaviour has been learned in circumstances which were gratifying.

This gratification is less easily available to the maladjusted person than to the normal. A person is said to be maladjusted when he shows a disproportionate preoccupation with problems which most people take in their stride. In a social context this preoccupation will show itself in either of two ways. On the one hand, the person may withdraw from social contacts because they take up time, energy, and attention which he cannot spare. On the other hand, he may seek out others in an attempt to express his troubles and be healed, as a sick cat looks for grass to eat. But this may be an unsuccessful manœuvre because, by now, his troubles may be such that self-expression and the sympathetic response of others does not suffice to help him: he may need professional advice. If this is so, he is not clear of his problem once he has expressed it, and he will return to it again and again in conversation. This places rather a heavy burden on most normal friendship-groups, let alone on a task-performing group, and the sufferer will come to be shunned. Thus, whichever social form maladjustment takes, it tends to produce isolation and rejection.

A consequence is that he has less opportunity for self-expression, although perhaps he needs more. When he sees that, contrary to the expectations earlier acquired, his self-expression is not welcomed by others, and not gratifying to them, he may withdraw, and hesitate to express himself. He will now fear to join groups, because he fears to be rejected. In this way, social hunger is created.

Consider by contrast the social and emotional functions of the expression of distressing experiences for a normal member. The occurrence of anything unusual in the life of a member provides the group with a break in routine. On hearing an account of it, the others enjoy the thrill of the experience without the unpleasantness that would have been their lot had they been personally involved. In his turn, the individual is compensated by the sympathy and interest with which the group receives his tale. For a moment, he is in the limelight. In this way, for those with an adequate social life, the group provides at least one compensation after a shock—an adult social substitute for the child's 'kissing it better'. The adult says: 'It does you good to talk.'

Self-expression is thus, to a mild extent, healing. In formal terms, self-expression serves an 'abreactive' or 'cathartic' function. The expectation that it will do so enables us to account for the irruption of self-expressive behaviour into a task-related sequence. On the other hand, self-expression enables the group to exercise control.

Self-expression and manifest social control

The group takes an interest in the emotional ups and downs of its members, but interest in any event lessens and after sufficient repetition disappears. A time comes when the group has heard the tale often enough. If this coincides with the moment at which the individual feels himself sufficiently compensated by the sympathetic response which he has received, all is well. The point at which abreaction ceases to be permitted is itself socially determined and would make an interesting study. But whatever the social background, a point must finally come when, if the sufferer insists on continuing his claims for attention, he will be regarded as a bore. He is no longer encouraged to express himself, but to forget it and get on with life. If he is capable of doing so, he will take the hint. The group has become, in Klapman's words, 'repressive-inspirational'.

Self-expression and social ignorance

Maladjustment is characterized by behaviour and values which differ from those current in society. Because his symptoms are so obtrusive, the maladjusted person may have been rejected before he had a chance to show where he was like-minded. He may thereby have lost touch to such an extent that he is no longer certain what is not permissible or, very much more often, what is perfectly all right. For people tend to avoid anyone who seems to them peculiar, without telling him why. In the therapeutic group (as also in a really good friendship group) such a person is given another chance. Whereas in daily life a wrong step in a social relationship may be irreparable, in a therapeutic group it meets with discussion and interpretation. The offender is acknowledged to be in the wrong, but this does not here involve his being cut off from the group. Nor is he now committed to maintain his direction for ever. There is not the same need for consistency. In this new and more permissive group he can try out new expressions of himself in the hope of discovering where he needs to change before he is acceptable to others, and which attempts at change are the successful ones. In this way he can become less ignorant socially.

Self-expression therefore leads to clarification. Sometimes when talking his problems over, the individual himself sees what needs to be done; sometimes he needs the guidance of others before he can see his situation more clearly. Part of this process consists, for reasons which will be discussed at length below, in a comparison of one's own practices with those of others. The following examples, reported by Kellmer Pringle, are taken from some parent-staff discussions with a Psychiatric Social Worker at a Remedial Education Centre.

(i) Mrs B had grossly over-protected her son who had remained very dependent on her, unable to mix with other boys and very retarded in all schoolwork. The question of children picking up undesirable accents or slang at school and whether parents should do anything deliberately to counteract this, was being discussed when Mrs B said: 'My biggest objection to following your advice [i.e. the P.S.W.'s] is just this: I cannot see any good from letting my Billy mix with the sort of children there are at his school.' Mr I: 'But can you prevent a child from mixing at school?' Mrs B: 'Fortunately I need not do anything, my Billy is far too sensible to want to mix with such children.' Mrs M: 'What sort of children?' Mrs B: 'They always just go around in gangs, use bad language and play stupid games.' Mr K: 'Surely there must be some children with whom your boy would like to play?' Mrs B: 'We are such good friends and I can so much share his interests, I don't think he wants any.' Mr H: 'I think a child needs the company of his own age however well he gets on with grown-ups. I used to worry about the bad language but I can see with my oldest—he's just 12 now—he knows when to speak properly and when not to because other boys would laugh at him for talking posh.' Mr G: 'I had a cousin who as a boy was always buried in books, got a scholarship to Oxford, but never mixed with other boys. Brilliant man but still doesn't know how to get on with people. We were afraid we would have the same problem with our middle boy. He was very solitary and as soon as he got home, he'd go into a huddle. Now we have moved to another area, it's pretty rough but it's on account of my business, and his new school sent him to the Centre. Anyhow, he seems now to be surrounded with children whom we wouldn't choose for him to mix with. But we can't keep him in now, and he is improving so much in every way, we no longer mind.' Mrs B had at first been rather self-conscious at finding herself the centre of discussion; she seemed surprised that all those who spoke differed from her own point of view and supported the suggestions previously made to her by the P.S.W.

(ii) Mr L had proved difficult both in his interviews with the P.S.W. as well as in the group meetings. He remained resistive to suggestions and sceptical about the methods of the Centre, suspecting them as being a 'soft option' for his very intelligent son. The boy's difficulties were due partly to uninspired teaching but mainly to the father's constant unfavourable comparison with the conforming, less high-spirited and somewhat self-satisfied older sister. Both parents attended regularly but progress seemed slow. At the fourth discussion meeting a newcomer to the group raised a problem which clearly showed an attitude similar to Mr L's. Immediately Mr L spoke up, using arguments and giving advice almost identical with that he had so often received himself. Of this he seemed unaware but he closed by saying: 'My problem was very much like yours but now I realize where I have gone wrong.' Coming from another parent the advice offered carried additional weight and conviction.

Self-expression and indirect social control

These examples show how members of a group, as well as providing a sympathetic audience, clarifying, reassuring, comparing, also help in another way by exchanging ideas on what is right in given circumstances. They do this either directly, e.g. 'Can you prevent a child from mixing?' or indirectly, by saying what their own practice is, e.g. 'We can't keep him in now, and he is improving so much in every way, we no longer mind'.

It may not be immediately obvious that information about other people's practices is an indirect form of social control. Yet several considerations can justify this hypothesis. First, one must know what the socially acceptable practices are before one can conform. Secondly, in order to do things in a socially acceptable way one must know the techniques in detail. The parents in this example knew they were odd in some way, but they were not sure exactly how and where. When they hear in detail what the others do, they are able to see more clearly in what respects they differ. In this way, they also come to know what behaviour would be acceptable in this group, and possibly in the larger society. They now have the information necessary to alter their own practice if they wish. Social control always operates so as to make the members of a group resemble one another more closely; the more they resemble one another, the more likely they are to be acceptable.

Self-expression and social independence

It will be seen that the therapeutic group enables the individual member to experiment with the techniques of social behaviour he has picked up during his life inside and outside the group.

He is given the opportunity to find out which techniques are incompatible, which are ineffective, and which may be added or relinquished without strain. The group tolerates him while he tries out alternative ways until he finds what is congenial to him and acceptable to others. The behaviour acceptable to others may, when first tried out by the individual, be 'external' to him. Newly-learnt ways are consciously and effortfully adhered to and only later become unquestioned and habitual: 'internalized'. Paradoxically, having become part of the personality, they make the person less dependent on the group than he was before.

This leads to an important phase in his development. The tendency to seek common ground will be replaced by attempts to establish where he agrees and disagrees: it shows a decreasing anxiety to conform in all respects; it is a step towards emancipation. In this way the group enables the member to become more of an individual, more himself. It shows him the standards held by other members of the group, and while he is still making these his own he begins to realize that perfect conformity in behaviour cannot be found and is not worth the seeking.

When this stage is reached, a genuine contribution to group life can be made. The member is part of the group, yet independent enough not to need to acquiesce all the time; he is able to give purpose and direction to the group, to initiate activity as well as respond to the lead of others. He plays a distinct role in the group and imparts to it his characteristic flavour.

BIBLIOGRAPHY

The distinction between task-related and expressive interaction

Bion W. R., 'Experiences in groups', *Human Relations* I–IV (1948–51).

Jennings H. H., *Leadership and Isolation* (Longmans, London, 1950).

Homans G., *The Human Group*, op. cit., ch. 4.

Bales R. F., *Interaction Process Analysis*, op. cit.

Schachter S., *The Psychology of Affiliation* (Stanford U.P., California, 1959).

Group psychotherapy

Klapman J. W., *Group Psychotherapy* (Heinemann, London, 1948).

Bierer J. (ed.), *Therapeutic Social Clubs* (H. K. Lewis, London, 1949).

Slavson S. R., *Analytic Group Psychotherapy* (Columbia U.P., New York, 1950).

Corsini R. J., *Methods of Group Psychotherapy* (McGraw-Hill, New York, 1957).

Foulkes S. H. and Anthony E. J., *Group Psychotherapy* (Penguin, London, 1957).

Pringle M. L. K., 'An experiment in parent-staff group discussion', *Educational Review* IX (1956–7).

Sociological discussions of social control and deviance

Parsons T., *The Social System* (Tavistock Publications, London, 1952), chs. 7 ff.

Merton R. K., *Social Theory and Social Structure* (Free Press, Illinois, 1957), ch. 5, ss. iv–v.

6

THE SOCIAL SIGNIFICANCE OF
SELF-EXPRESSION

There are three types of self-expressive behaviour: friendliness, hostility and withdrawal from interaction. Friendliness is a sign of satisfaction in group-membership, of satisfaction with other members, and of satisfaction with task-performance. It therefore has a cohesive function. Personality considerations apart, friendliness is accorded to those who share the outlook of the members, and especially to those who exemplify it. In this way also, friendliness has a cohesive function. Friendliness is not extended to those who, by expressing friendliness on inappropriate occasions, show that they do not share the group's ideas. Those who cannot agree tend to withdraw from interaction with one another except when circumstances compel them to remain. When membership of deviants is enforced, hostility will occur. Hostility and withdrawal are disruptive, but the fear of such negative self-expression may serve a cohesive function. The expectation of rejection is a means of social control. Self-expressive behaviour tends to construct and maintain social reality in the group.

EXPRESSIVE behaviour may be regarded from two points of view: what it does for the individual and what it does for the group. The previous chapter gave an indication of what it does for the individual: it satisfies the social hunger it first created, it corrects social ignorance, and in both ways it acts as a form of social control. In this chapter individual self-expression is to be considered in relation to its effects on the group. These effects can be discussed in parallel terms of group-attractiveness and cohesion on the one hand, and of social control on the other, for generally speaking the greater the attraction which the group has for its members, the more cohesive the group will be and the greater the control it can exercise over

4

the behaviour of individual members. This being so, our problem is to define the circumstances in which self-expression makes the group more attractive, more cohesive, more authoritative to its members, and contrast with these the occasions on which self-expression will have the opposite effect. This problem is flanked by two others, so that the three questions we must ask ourselves are: What forms of self-expression may be observed in the group? In which circumstances will each form strengthen or disrupt the group? And how are any conclusions we come to on these questions to be verified?

The first question can be answered quite simply and, for the moment, arbitrarily. The observation-schedule will allow three categories of expressive behaviour: friendliness, hostility, and withdrawal. In the course of the discussion which now follows, the reason for their selection should appear: they enable us to define types of cohesive and disruptive acts in the group; they fit in with research-conclusions on the nature of social control; and existing techniques of measurement can be couched in the terms we use. In this way, work on different aspects of small-group studies can be organized to form a consistent whole. At the end of the chapter we shall return to the problem of social ignorance, but this time with the emphasis on the intellectual and task-performing side, rather than its emotional side.

Before we consider the expressive categories in relation to mechanisms of social control, a word may be said on how they relate to one another. Friendliness has as its opposite unfriendliness, which may manifest itself either as hostility or as withdrawal from interaction. Withdrawal from interaction has interaction as its opposite, which may be either friendly or hostile. Hostility is an aggressive reaction; this element of aggression is absent from the other two forms of expressive behaviour. We may now consider each in turn.

Friendliness

The occasions on which friendly behaviour occurs can be deduced from what was said in the previous chapter. When the individual expresses ideas of which the group approves, this is felt by the other members to be a friendly act and therefore they respond with friendly expressions on their part. Friendliness thus keeps the group attractive and cohesive in that it strengthens the feeling of belonging and acceptability which is one of the basic satisfactions of group-membership.

Friendliness may also occur spontaneously whenever a member is happy and at home in the group. This indicates to others that he likes the group, and is therefore gratifying to them (except in special circumstances to be discussed below). Thirdly, friendliness may occur as a morale-raising attempt when there is a danger that the group will lose its attraction for some member. Chapter 11 gives an example of a member who, having expressed unpopular ideas and been attacked for them, is later the recipient of much friendly behaviour; presumably this reassures him about his acceptability in the group and prevents his withdrawal. Finally, friendliness may mark the successful completion of a task. Bales and his associates have demonstrated that the problem-solving sequence tends to end with such self-expressive behaviour. There is evidence to suggest that members who have been associated with the successful performance of a task are thereafter better liked, and that a group which is successful is regarded as more attractive by its actual and by prospective members. In addition to this normal increase in friendly expression at the end of a successfully performed task and in unfriendly expression at the end of a less successfully performed task, the members may have 'stored up' friendly expressions which they regarded as irrelevant while the task was as yet unfinished.

Admiration and popularity

The cohesive function of mutually friendly self-expression between equals is thus established. But friendliness is not spread equally over all members. No member likes all the others equally well. The occasions on which one member shows his likings for another must of course depend to some extent on whether the one is a friendly person in general and the other likable. That is, it depends to some extent on personality-variables outside the scope of group-studies. Yet much remains to be said within our terms of reference.

Consider the glow of pleasure we feel whenever someone else says what we would have liked to say, or does what we would have liked to do, rather better than we could. This is partly due to gratification that our ideas are shared by someone else. Rightly or wrongly, such sharing seems to confirm their validity: it creates a 'social reality'. Moreover, among the ideas are values and ideals, and these are in the nature of aspirations. They represent not what we are but what we would like to be, are at our best, when most pleased with ourselves. Accordingly, when others behave more frequently or more steadily in this way, they are bound to be admired: they exemplify the ideas we cherish.

Admittedly, human nature is a little more complicated than this. Even in quite task-related impersonal groups, members will show more than one side of their personality. Unless the members are really implausibly similar, each will conform more to some of the group's norms than to others. In some circumstances they will appear more admirable than they would in other circumstances, and for much the same reasons, they will appear more admirable to some members than to others. This argument by no means invalidates the general hypothesis that the more a member conforms, the more he is approved; it only sophisticates it. Riley and Cohn, for instance, argue that a man is praised by his friends for his conformity to some norms of the group; if his enemies want to criticize him, they do so by blaming him for his deviance from certain other of the group's norms. A member is, therefore, kept on the rails in two ways: by being rewarded by his friends when he conforms and by being blamed by his enemies when he does not.

So the individual finds himself in a network of social relations, giving friendliness to those who are nearest to him in outlook but slightly superior, and receiving friendliness from those to whom he is nearest in outlook and slightly superior.

Both types of relationship are attractive to him and therefore cohesive in function.

Unfriendliness: hostility and withdrawal

Basically, then, friendliness depends on the expression or exemplification of approved ideas, and this is easily related to cohesiveness. But sometimes ideas are expressed which are not shared or approved by the group. These ideas may be concerned with task-performance and to that extent they will be considered in later chapters. There is, however, an interesting special case which belongs properly to the present discussion. Even friendly self-expression is not always approved by the group. An example of this was already encountered in the previous chapter by the maladjusted in his quest for a group which would not reject him. Similarly, a more or less normal individual may be disappointed and surprised to find that he has too optimistically carried over into a new group the ideas and behaviour which stood him in good stead in earlier groups of which he had experience. He may, for instance, inappropriately engage in self-expression as a means of establishing his own worth and that of other members. That is: he engages in this behaviour when he should be engaged in task-related activity or he engages in behaviour which in an earlier group would have affirmed a shared way of life, but which does not do so in his present group.

Strictly speaking, there is only one source of inappropriateness: unshared ideas. For a man to engage in self-expression when others are busy on the task demonstrates that the task is less important to him than to the others. Inappropriateness therefore is caused by social ignorance: by not knowing what is considered right in the group in which one finds oneself.

What is likely to be the consequence of the expression of unshared ideas? This depends on a number of variables. Often the first consequence is that the members will attempt to persuade the deviant by (what they imagine to be) rational persuasion. There is therefore often a phase immediately after the discovery of deviance in which more interaction is directed at the deviant than at the ordinary members of the group. In so far as this persuasion is rational, it will be discussed in chapter 10. Such persuasion may also have expressive aspects. At first deviants may be made a fuss of. This may be a friendly fuss; they will be called interesting and refreshing. Unless they change their ways, however, this will not last.

When finally the group discovers that the deviant is not going to change his ways or his ideas, the members will effect an abrupt *withdrawal of interaction* with the deviant. Stubborn deviants are regarded as not belonging properly to the group.

If, therefore, there is no important reason for keeping all the members together, the group will split, falling apart along lines determined by adherence to particular forms of behaviour, or by adherence to people exemplifying them. Examples may be found in chapter 7. If only one member deviates, he may simply not bother to turn up at the next meeting, or he may find that the group takes steps to make life sufficiently unpleasant for him to withdraw. This is a common experience among those who find themselves in the therapeutic groups discussed in the previous chapter.

If, however, there are good reasons why the group should not disintegrate, the members will try very hard to overcome the discrepancy in outlook between the contending parties. For *hostility* is inevitable if the group has to continue in being with incompatible members in it. This is likely to happen when the task is considered by all to be important, or when the members are forced to remain together by some outside agency, which may in addition reward conformity or punish non-conformity.

As a first conclusion we may say that hostility and withdrawal are disruptive forms of self-expression, which occur as a symptom of some incompatibility of outlook in the group. For manifest expressions, this is indeed the case. There is, however, one important qualification to be made to this generalization. As Homans has pointed out, the fear that disruptive forms of self-expression may occur acts often as a cohesive mechanism, as a form of social control which he calls 'virtual' control. Before a member starts something

new, while he is yet considering, he will take into account
the possibility that his relationship with the group will be
adversely affected, and this may check him before he starts.
In this way, the common outlook of the group is preserved
and cohesion maintained, by virtue of the possibility of
disruption.

The relationship between conformity (the absence of social
ignorance), cohesion (the absence of social hunger), and
social control is not a simple one. At the same time that an
appreciation of the group's standards gives the individual a
desire to belong, the desire to belong gives the individual an
incentive to alter his ideas and behaviour. But perception of a
group's standards is by no means always accurate, especially
to an individual who is still outside. He may desire membership because he perceives patterns of behaviour which he
admires, without being aware that they are of only secondary
importance to established members, and he may be ignorant of
certain other patterns to which he will be expected to conform
when he has joined: he may not always know in which direction
he is moving.

To sum up: the group has power over the individual in proportion to his need to belong. If he is unwilling to share the
group's outlook, he will be rejected or he must withdraw.
He must conform in areas the group considers important, as
well as in areas attractive to him as an individual. The more
important the group considers the area to be, the greater will
be the pressure on him to conform. The more important a
member the group considers him to be, the greater the pressure. The more cohesive the group, the more intense the efforts
to keep it so, and the greater the possibility of rejection when
he deviates. To some of the less desirable consequences of
this process we will return at the end of this chapter.

A great deal of empirical evidence is available to confirm
the theories of behaviour discussed in the present chapter.
This evidence depends on a useful technique for measuring
the social and emotional relationships in the group: *sociometry*.

Moreno, the inventor of sociometry, started with the fact

that friendliness is not spread equally over all members. This inequality becomes apparent when each member is asked to choose another member to share with him in certain activities. The ever-recurring distinction between task-related and expressive behaviour must here be taken into account once again. Sociometry distinguishes between socio-groups and psyche-groups. Psyche-group structure shows up when the members are asked to make choices for activities not related to a common task, for instance: 'With whom would you like to go to the pictures?' or 'Whom do you want sitting next to you at dinner?' Socio-group structure reveals a preferred task-structure. It may be found by asking a member of a drama group with whom he wants to act, or a member of a flying group with whom he wants to fly. If members are presented with both kinds of question, different structures emerge in response to each—one group: two structures. It is also interesting to note once again the primacy of expressive behaviour: unless members are given sufficient opportunity of choosing to be with those they like, they will choose their friends to work with them at tasks for which they may not be suitable.

The charted replies to these questions will show a number of *isolates* (individuals not chosen by anyone), some *mutual choices*, and some *stars* (individuals chosen by many others). The number of isolates, mutual choices and stars which one would expect if people chose each other at random can be mathematically ascertained. In established groups we find that the actual distribution differs significantly from a random model. This we may justly attribute to the flow of sentiments in the group.

One later refinement of the method enables us to distinguish not only between the recipients of friendliness and those who are left out of consideration, but also those who are rejected. Another refinement allows us to find out what the members imagine their own sociometric position in the group to be. This is achieved by asking members to say by whom they expect to be chosen.

An imaginary example will show the kind of organization

likely to emerge upon the questions: 'With whom would you like to go to the pictures?' and 'Name someone with whom you would like least to go to the pictures.' Only one choice is assumed to have been permitted in answer to each of these questions. (The structure might look very different if more than one choice were allowed, but it would look a little more confusing.) Positive choices are shown by continuous lines, negative choices by broken lines.

A sociogram showing friendliness, hostility and withdrawal

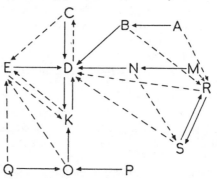

Friendliness. It will be noticed that the number of mutual choices is small in this group. Only R and S, and D and K, are each other's first choice. One of these friendly couples, R and S, is quite isolated from the group as far as friendship is concerned: those who are aware of their existence dislike them. The other couple, D and K, is a focus of friendship for the group. D is the star: he is the recipient of five choices directly, and of a number of others through friendly intermediaries.

Popularity. The sociogram shows that friendliness in a group may be rather one-sided. More people love Tom Fool than Tom Fool loves. D is emotionally dependent on K only. Five members depend on him. This suggests that a dependence-relationship rather than a mutually equal relationship may come into being between a star and other members of the group. This may be more characteristic of groups with some kind of imbalance. Bion, for instance, working with therapeutic groups, was so much struck by this characteristic that instead of the conventional division into friendliness, hostility, and withdrawal, he uses the categories of 'flight-and-fight', 'pairing', and 'dependence'. In other words, withdrawal and hostility (flight-and-fight) are grouped together as basically one form of behaviour, and a distinction is made between sexually-tinged friendliness (pairing) and exploitative friendliness (dependence). For our purposes, which are more to do with task-related groups, we shall see this exploitative friendliness as realistically conceived in terms of promotion, power, and prestige. For this reason a further discussion is postponed to chapter 8.

Hostility. There is only one couple of members who are mutually averse, K and E. E is, as it were, a dark star: the recipient of a large number of negative choices. R and S, who are mutual friends, are also the recipients of a number of negative choices. It may be significant that they unite in a dislike of the great star, D.

Withdrawal. Finally, there are a number of members who are not thought of by the others at all, either with warmth or with hostility: they are likely to be only peripherally important to the group; their approval or their disapproval will not matter, their contribution to the group will be lightly regarded. P is the most obvious example; A, M, and Q are in much the same case.

Jennings' comparison of the characteristics of girls who were chosen in a sociometric test markedly more often than could be accounted for by chance (the 'over-chosen') with the characteristics of girls who received an average number of choices provides us with a striking confirmation of the theories expounded in this chapter. The over-chosen girls showed, among other characteristics:

a. *three times* as much initiatory behaviour in making innovations with or without permission, as did girls receiving an average number of choices, *b. twice* as much planning and organization,

c. four times as much initiative in planning new projects,

d. four times as much behaviour exhibiting ingenuity in changing the conduct of problem-members, or fostering understanding between new members and others,

e. twice the incidences of rebellious behaviour.

On the other hand, the under-chosen showed:

a. twelve times as often, incidences of interfering with the group's activities,

b. five times as much quarrelsomeness and irritability,

c. eleven times as much behaviour pernicious in its effect on the group (spreading false rumours, etc.).

How is this to be explained?

It is obvious that the under-chosen interfered with what the group wanted to do. The over-chosen, the 'stars', exhibited more kindliness and sense, which is a good reason for liking anyone. But this example has been chosen because it provides a telling illustration of our general argument. How are these stars' rebelliousness and enterprise in disobedience to be accounted for? The answer: these were delinquent girls in a reformatory! Bowing before authority, and keeping within the constraints imposed thereby, would not be highly thought of by these girls; therefore the leaders would be girls who could demonstrate that these authority-values were not theirs. The stars express the values of the group to a greater extent than the other girls. The literature on this subject is full of examples of a less obviously impressive kind.

Social reality, social consensus, and group autism

Jennings' study illustrates not only the relationship between conformity and expressive behaviour; it also illustrates that there are dangers in this relationship. Consider again the argument pursued in these last two chapters: social hunger goes together with social ignorance; group membership leads to social control; social control operates, in a terrifying variety of ways, to make the members more like-minded; to be like-minded is the surest guarantee of acceptance into a group. But there is no guarantee that the conformity a group procures is conformity to admirable values or testable facts. Conformity may be to *social reality* only.

Social reality is established by *social consensus*: by the group's agreement on what is true or false, right or wrong, relevant or irrelevant. Watson has put this well:

> It is a commonplace to point out that a complex society like our own is inevitably ambiguous. Reality cannot be fully known by perceiving it, and so it becomes known by definition. A major function of sociability is to provide acceptable explanations for aspects of the external world which are either puzzling or threatening. When the criterion for accuracy cannot be correspondence with observed facts, it becomes correspondence with social reality, which is to say, the judgements of one's friends.

Social reality is, to the members who share it, factual reality. But when social and factual reality are identified instead of contrasted, a danger arises. Ideas which everyone shares—or at least, which no one contradicts—are likely to be accepted as true ideas. Festinger writes: 'To the extent that objective, non-social means are not available, people evaluate their opinions and abilities by comparison with the opinions and abilities of others.'

This is as relevant to the ideas exchanged at a task-related level as it is to expressive interaction. For obvious reasons this point was glossed over in the discussion on task-related behaviour in chapter 3. But we may now ask ourselves, how do we know when an intellectual task has been satisfactorily performed? The answer is that we must assume that the solution of an intellectual task is reached when all members agree that a solution has been reached. This is for most purposes a fair enough assumption. Reaching agreement when members start with different presuppositions is no mean achievement. And if a solution cannot be tested at once, social consensus—i.e. the agreement that if one were to test the solution it would prove to be the correct one—is as much as one can hope to achieve. Thus what is often called, in formal meetings, 'establishing the facts' may turn out to be solely an agreement that these are the facts. Social consensus establishes social reality.

In this way, social reality exerts a powerful pressure to conform, even when there is no obviously social motive for conformity. If everyone in the group is agreed that a member's ideas are mistaken, and there is no way of checking up, that member is almost bound to believe that he is in the wrong. He will change his mind and come more closely into line with the ideas current in his group. The benign aspects of this process were sufficiently illustrated when the clarificatory function of the therapeutic group was discussed in the previous chapter.

But the process is not necessarily benign. There are at least two dangers. The first, illustrated by Jennings, Schrag and others, is that the group's values may not be culturally respectable. In this way we can speak of the social reality of a criminal sub-culture. The second danger is that the more inward-looking the group is, the less the members will be in contact with reality as it appears to others. In so far as they then find themselves unable to agree with 'outsiders', they will withdraw from further interaction if they can, and feel hostility if they cannot. The outsiders will, of course, reciprocate for the same reasons. This has been called 'group-autism'. Now if the social reality of the in-group happens to be accurately conceived, its members will lose touch with the rest of society, possibly to the extent of being unable to make a useful contribution to the life of all. And if their social reality happens to be inaccurately conceived, they will lose the ability to adapt creatively to their surroundings. Scientists, artists, clergy, politicians are among the groups who have at times been accused of one or other of these faults.

BIBLIOGRAPHY

Friendliness, hostility, and withdrawal as interaction-categories

Joel W. and Shapiro D., 'Some principles and procedures for group psychotherapy', *J. Psych.* XXXIX, 1950.

Bion W. R., 'Experiences in groups', op. cit.

The popularity of members useful to task-performance

Deutsch M., 'The effects of co-operation and competition on group process', *Human Relations* II (1949) and abridged in Cartwright and Zander, op. cit.

Gilchrist J. G., 'The formation of social groups under conditions of success and failure', *J. Abnormal and Social Psych.* XLVII (1952).

Berkovitz L. *et al.* 'Effects of performance-evaluation on group integration and motivation', *Human Relations* X (1957).

Friendly interaction following on successful task-performance

Bales R. F., *Interaction Process Analysis*, op. cit., pp. 126–36.

Bales R. F. and Strodtbeck F. L., 'Phases in group problem-solving' (1951), in Cartwright and Zander, op. cit., ch. 26.

Parsons T., Bales R. F. and Shils E., *Working Papers in the Theory of Action*, op. cit., chs. 3–5.

Heinicke C. and Bales R. F., 'Developmental trends in the structure of small groups', *Sociometry* XVI (1953).

Friendliness, hostility, and withdrawal as means of control

French J. R. P., 'The disruption and cohesion of groups' (1941), in Cartwright and Zander, op. cit., ch. 10.

Thibaut J., 'An experimental study of the cohesiveness of under-privileged groups' (1950), in Cartwright and Zander, op. cit., ch. 9.

Schachter S., 'Deviation, communication and rejection' (1951), in Cartwright and Zander, op. cit., ch. 17.

Back K., 'Influence through social communication', *J. Abnormal and Social Psych.* XLVI (1951).

Festinger L. *et al*, 'The influence process in the presence of extreme deviates', *Human Relations* V (1952).

Gerard H. B., 'The effects of different dimensions of disagreement on the communication process', *Human Relations* VI (1953).

Gerard H. B., 'The anchorage of opinions in face-to-face groups', *Human Relations* VII (1953).

Klein J., *The Study of Groups* (Routledge, London, 1956), ch. 10.

Coser L., *The Functions of Social Conflict* (Routledge, London, 1956).

Israel J., *Self-evaluation and Rejection in Groups* (Almqvist and Wiksell, Uppsala, 1956).

Cartwright D. and Zander A., *Group Dynamics*, op. cit., pt.2.

Goffman E., 'Alienation from interaction', *Human Relations* X (1957).

Riley M. W. and Cohn, R., 'Control networks in informal groups'. *Sociometry* XXI (1958).

Sociometry

Moreno J. L., *Who Shall Survive?* (Beacon House, New York, 1943),

Jennings H. H., *Leadership and Isolation*, op. cit.

Tagiuri R., 'Relational analysis: an extension of sociometric method with emphasis on social perception', Hare, Borgatta and Bales, op. cit., ch. 5.

Lindzey G. and Borgatta E. F., 'Sociometric Measurement', Lindzey G. (ed.) *Handbook of Social Psychology* (Wiley, New York, 1954), ch. 11.

The journal *Sociometry*.

Social reality, social consensus and group autisms

Allport F. H., 'The influence of the group upon association and thought', *J. Exper. Psych.* III (1920).

Jenness A., 'The role of discussion in changing opinion regarding matters of fact', *J. Abnormal and Social Psych.* XXVII (1932).

Chapman D. W. and Volkman J., 'A social determinant of the level of aspiration' (1939), in Newcomb (ed.), *Readings in Social Psychology* (Holt, New York, 1947).

Festinger L., 'Factors influencing the level of aspiration', *J. Abnormal and Social Psych.* XXXVII (1942).

Newcomb T. M., 'Autistic hostility and social reality', *Human Relations* I (1948).

Sherif M., *An Outline of Social Psychology* (Harper, New York, 1948), chs. 6–8.

Asch S. E., 'Effects of group pressure on the modification and distortion of judgements' (1951), in Cartwright and Zander, op. cit., ch. 12.

Festinger L., 'A theory of the social comparison process', Hare, Borghatta and Bales, op. cit.

Schrag C., 'Leadership among prison inmates', *Amer. Sociol. Review* XIX (1954).

Blake R. R. *et al*, 'Gift-giving as a function of group standards', *Human Relations* VIII (1955).

Ziller R. C., 'Scales of judgement: a determinant of the accuracy of group decision', *Human Relations* VIII (1955).

Israel J., *Self-evaluation and Rejection in Groups*, op. cit.

Klein J., *The Study of Groups*, op. cit., ch. 6.

Watson J., 'A formal analysis of social interaction', *Sociometry* XXI (1958).

7

GROUPS IN THEIR FORMAL AND INFORMAL ENVIRONMENT

The ideas which members import into the group have usually been acquired in other groups. These other groups provide the formal and informal setting for a committee's deliberations. They may therefore act as pressure-groups. In this way, the functions of the members are limited by the formal and informal groupings to which they belong: both as regards facts and as regards values. Consequently, the interaction-process is affected by the social environment of the group: not all the feasible solutions to a problem will be considered or acceptable in the group.

IT IS not to be supposed that the social psychologist is the only one to realize the importance of social pressures for the creation of social consensus. Many committees owe their *raison d'être* to this knowledge.

Committees are decision-making groups in their purest form. A committee works best when personal considerations enter least into its deliberations. But even when personal considerations are absent, and each member confines himself as strictly to the task as is humanly possible, there is no reason to suppose that there will be harmony of views and speedy agreement on the best course of action.

The reason for this is to be found partly in the very purpose for which committees are set up. They tend to exist in a formal framework of large organizations. These organizations may require the performance of a task which would be best carried out by a group especially created for the purpose. For instance, a number of interests may have to be consulted if informed co-operation in the execution of a plan is to be ensured. The committee members will, each of them, have been selected because they were able to contribute the necessary information or to insist on the right values. Each is there as a delegate from a larger social grouping which trusts him to 'represent its interests'.

This trust is partly based on an expectation of loyalty, but the unconscious absorption of information and values which results from the delegate's membership of the larger social grouping exerts an equally important pressure. The way in which membership of primary groups impresses ideas on the individual is reproduced, though in a milder form, in the pressure exerted by a formal organization upon the ideas of its members. Each is therefore likely to import into the committee's decisions those considerations which affect the group which sent him, and to export information which his group of origin requires. He will also come with certain expectations as to what the best decision will be, his best deriving from what he knows before he enters and therefore closely connected with the best of the group he is representing. Personal considerations apart, he is to this extent partial. Similar considerations govern his expectation as to what his role will be.

Since this is equally true for each member of the group, each will also come with expectations about the probable behaviour and role of others in the group—expectations which he bases on his beliefs about the organizations or informal groupings which they represent: the information the others are likely to possess and the values the others are likely to stress.

Even if we eliminate differences in personal qualities, therefore, we should expect some members to be regarded with greater respect or with greater caution, before anyone even opens his mouth. Expectations concerning one's own role and those concerning the roles of others are thus mutually interdependent. And these expectations, in so far as the member does not behave purely expressively, determine the form and the content of his interaction: what he says, why he says it, to whom he says it; to whom he listens, whom he ignores, and why. Certain aspects of task-performance and certain directions of thought will be inhibited by the setting in which the group exists, and the contribution that any member can make will be similarly delimited and defined.

When a group is formally part of a larger organization, the relationship between that group and others is often laid down in a constitution, an organizational charter, a law, or some other terms of reference, which may also be represented by a chart. The chart will show how the task and membership of any particular group is limited to a certain extent by the existence of other groups. It should not be forgotten, however, that a chart is only a model of the way the organization should work; it does not take into account the more human failings, and it does not allow for the growth and change of groups.

Chart of persons, groups and committees within an industrial organization

Charts can also be constructed to show how various organizations intermesh in a particular group. Such charts will throw light on the probable function of each member.

Chart to show the position of a sub-committee relative to other organizations

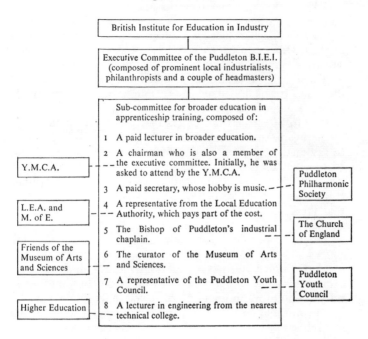

In this way, any group may be seen as the place where a lot of other groups are in contact with one another. The group is in this respect a kind of market-place where other groups can exchange information and views concerning relative values. If we focus on the 'market-place' group, we can see that ideas are being imported by virtue of each member's other affiliations. If we focus on the groups outside, we can see that information will also be exported to them; values are perhaps exported to a lesser extent. The knowledge of a member's affiliations with other groups enables one to predict with some confidence what values and what information he can or will import; for the first time, we can predict something about the content of interaction. Such a member can of course also be used at times to export ideas in the hope of influencing the social environment. The group is not only subjected to pressure; it can at times operate as a pressure-group.

The exchange of ideas is a consequence of any inter-group contact. Other consequences spring from the differing ability of various groups to make an impact: they differ in the extent to which their views have to be taken into consideration when decisions are made. Members are bound to see some of the outside groups as 'above' them in the sense that the outsiders can control their destiny; others they can see as 'below'; and others again as parallel or irrelevant. On the whole it is true to say of those higher up that they have access to more, and to more inaccessible, information, and that they can make decisions with wider implications, which will affect those below them. They can also insist in certain circumstances that the group must work towards ends which they wish to further.

On the other hand, one may also say—though it is less often said—that decisions made at lower levels have a bearing on current high-level considerations. The actions of subordinates cannot be ignored and cannot be constantly overruled. Moreover, those at lower levels have often valuable 'inside information': they will know more about some aspects of routine and about the problems which arise from the day-to-day running of the establishment. This kind of information is often extremely relevant to the practicability or desirability of a plan decided upon at a higher level.

It is therefore a salutary exercise for the newcomer to any committee to ask himself certain questions: Why was he co-opted (or elected)? Are his own expectations of how he will contribute shared by the committee? What are the committee's expectations of his function? Is he going to perform on exactly the same lines as his predecessor, and if not, will the committee be disappointed, alarmed, or gratified? Is his place on the committee to be regarded as a concession to some special interest, and do some hope that he will be a quietening sop to a local Cerberus? Or do all recognize that he is coming to fill a gap, a felt need? In what respects, and by whom, is innovation likely to be welcomed? In what respects, and by whom, is conformity expected? Where are the 'growing points'? How can he best exercise his special talent within the existing framework? The answer to such questions can to some extent be found by a thoughtful examination of the formal setting within which the committee must do its work.

Generally speaking, anything that is happening at one level of an organization may affect people operating at other levels. For this reason charts are informative to a new man entering a group, for from them he may tell who is above him, relying on his work, and whom he must consult on matters outside or overlapping his own sphere of competence. Similarly, he can tell who, below him, has to execute the decisions he makes, and who may therefore have information concerning day-to-day aspects which should affect his decisions. He will be able to see the position of other members in his group in relation to their superiors and subordinates as well as his own, and he will know where these coincide or overlap. To some extent he will be able to tell where, in the formal structure, support or opposition will be found for a variety of proposals. The task, and the contribution a member is permitted to make to it, is thus formally delimited and defined.

We have now dealt with two aspects of role-structure. First, there is that aspect of structure which is the outcome of each member contributing in the best possible way to the task-performance of the group—as expert, as facilitator, as co-ordinator, or as morale-builder. This may be called the *rational-ideal structure*. Secondly, there is that aspect of organization which is formally determined by some outside agency or by the formal setting in which the group exists. This is called the *formal structure*.

A third aspect has now to be considered. There is also that distribution of function, not necessarily similar to either of the above, which a task-performing group finds most congenial. When the formal organization is such that members cannot conveniently work with it, they may produce an *informal structure* which they consider more suited to the task and to the group. The informal structure may, however, approximate to the rational-ideal no more than the formal structure did. For one thing, awareness and experience are necessary before a group can spontaneously perceive and perform the roles necessary for good task-performance and high morale. Moreover, it is not always easy to remain task-related after the frustrating experience of finding that the formal rules do not work. And lastly, the formal context provides only part of the environment for any group. Informal pressures are also brought to bear on the definition of task and role.

The world outside, and in particular other informal groupings, will be bound to affect informal behaviour in the group. This is of course true for committees, but it is of equal interest when observing interaction in discussion-groups or debates. No group can avoid the informal pressures and alignments which result from a consensus of ideas in groupings only tangentially related to it: party-political allegiances, the mutual mistrust between young and old, the antagonisms between the up-and-coming and the establishment, and so on. Members of a group who find themselves on the same side of such dividing lines share certain ideas to which they attach importance. Alignments are produced by (and also produce) common views among those on the same side. This means that they may also find themselves in sympathy when it comes to views on the best way to perform the task or on the member best qualified to perform it. Certain conclusions will appear obvious to them. The facts and values they take into consideration may be unstated and taken for granted by them, but not by the other side, which will therefore view their proposals with (possibly unwarranted) scepticism. Similarly the confidence they place in the ability of a member of their own sub-group may seem misplaced to those outside. A sociometric star is by definition a star only to his own group. Inevitably, therefore, the ideas put forward by one man will undergo more stringent examination than will those of another man whose ideas are more closely shared.

In these ways, informal and unorganized pressures are at work in the group, in some ways strengthening, and in other ways modifying, the structures formally intended. The task, and the contribution a member is permitted to make, is thus further delimited and defined.

In the two examples which follow, the formal setting has determined the broad outlines of task and role-structure; the informal setting defines within narrower limits how the task is performed and what co-operation is achieved. These are students' descriptions which make no consistent attempt to distinguish between the effects of the formal context and the effects of the informal context, but this will nevertheless be clear to the reader.

Description of social relations in an Approved School

The description which follows shows some implications and consequences of a group structure whose setting could be charted thus:

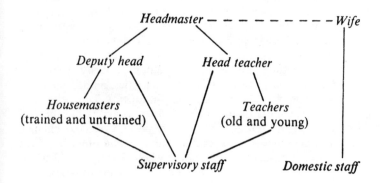

Like most Approved Schools this school was in an isolated position, 5 miles from the nearest town. Most of the staff lived either in or near the school, which meant that a great deal of their lives was shared, and relationships were more intimate. In such circumstances subgroups tend to be more pronounced and rivalries more noticeable.

As can be seen from the chart, apart from the four senior personnel, there emerge four main subgroups.

1. *Housemasters:* The boys were split into three houses, each with a housemaster. Attached to each house were some teaching staff and supervisory staff, but, apart from relationships with boys, the staff attached to each house never became a group. The housemasters as such were a closed group, they were not actually in the life of the school till after school hours. They did not discuss the boys' home circumstances or background. They attended case-meetings, which the teaching staff did not. On the whole the group was separate from the teachers, except for one younger, and trained, housemaster, who mixed far more with the younger teachers. This became a subgroup on its own, with views on discipline and routine for the boys, which differed from those of the older staff. There was a good deal of sympathetic interaction between housemasters and supervisory staff; this was mainly because they were responsible to the housemaster for supervision duty.

2. *The Teachers:* This group was a distinct one, subdivided in the main between old and young. As a group they had their common grouse about housemasters: the lack of work they apparently have, their attendance at case-meetings, and their apparent superiority. (For they were in charge of out-of-school activities, and they seemed to have more contact with authority.) Thus the subdivisions were on the one hand the older staff, who had been in the school for a long time and disliked changes and new methods of teaching, and on the other hand the younger element which, on the whole, soon wearied of the secluded atmosphere of the school and tried to break from

it as much as possible. They were also more keen to try out new ideas and experiments in the schoolroom, more active in sport, and therefore more popular with the boys. The distinction 'young and old' is here not applied so much to age as to ideology.

3. *The supervisory staff:* These were on the whole maintenance staff, etc., such as gardeners, carpenters, plumbers, who were expected to take supervisory duties in out-of-school activities. They generally had not much friction with other groups, but their contacts were mainly with the housemasters and the boys. On all points of welfare or out-of-school routine they would be expected to take the side of the housemasters.

4. *The domestic staff:* These had little dealing with the rest of the staff.

In the next example, the description has been phrased in terms of individual psychological traits. The social determinants of the alignments should nevertheless be clear even to the casual reader.

Description of social relations in a Civil Service section

Some subgroups come to exist through the personality peculiarities of individual members of staff. In this category perhaps the most important subgroup was caused by the totally unsuitable personality of the officer-in-charge for the job in question. He had been transferred from some obscure post in another Ministry, and knew nothing at all of the provisions of the Act under which we worked, let alone the difficulties of the department's staff in administering and executing those provisions. The effect was such as to turn all but one of the employees against him. Hence a feeling was produced of hostility from a very strong subgroup working totally out of touch with the officer-in-charge and his crony. The helpful personality of one of the executive officers, on the other hand, formed a subgroup

round him as a centre, with newer members of staff form-
ing a hard core in this subgroup.

BIBLIOGRAPHY

Festinger L., 'Belongingness in a voting situation', *Human Relations*
I (1948).

Sherif M. and Sherif C. W., *Groups in Harmony and Tension* (Harper,
New York, 1953), chs. 7–10.

Kelley H. H., 'Salience of membership and resistance to changes of
group-anchored attitudes', *Human Relations* VIII (1955).

Turner R. H., 'Role-taking, role-standpoint and reference-group
behaviour', *Amer. J. Sociol.* LXI (1955–56).

Gardner E. F. and Thompson G. G., *Social Relations and Morale
in Small Groups* (Appleton-Century-Crofts, New York, 1956).

Israel J., *Self-evaluation and Rejection in Groups*, op. cit.

Merton R. K., *Social Theory and Social Structure*, op. cit., ch. 8
(with Alice S. Rossi) and ch. 9.

Sofer C., 'Reactions to administrative change: a study of staff-
relations in three British hospitals', *Human Relations* VIII (1955).

8

INFLUENTIAL MEMBERS AND THEIR INFLUENCE

A member may be an opinion-leader by virtue of his expertise or his sociometric position. A member may also be an opinion-leader by virtue of his contacts with other groups which may be considered more important or less accessible. A member may become an opinion-leader if he has in the past made many decisions which the group approved as correct. Other members may over-estimate the importance of an opinion-leader in any of these respects. In formal organizations the values of the organization define the task and the task-structure of the group; the problem of effective organization and appointed leadership then arises. Formal organizations secure co-operation by providing rewards, by training in the values and skills of the organization; and by formal definition of the role-structure. The qualities of a good appointed leader in a formal organization are those of a good leader in a self-selected group.

DISCUSSIONS are intended to end in agreement. Ideally, agreement is secured when all members share the same values and see the facts at their disposal in the same light. In fact, however, some members find it easier than others to secure agreement. Such a member we shall call an opinion-leader. He may be recognized by the fact that when he states his ideas, other members support him; and when others give their views, the members wait for him to react before they respond.

In accordance with our theory, an opinion-leader may be an unusually able person recognized as an expert by other members, so that they put their trust in the information he places at their disposal and in the views he is supposed to base on that information. Whether he is thought unusually able depends of course to some extent on the group's social reality—although if he genuinely is so, the group would have to be very autistic indeed if it does not in the end recognize him to be so, regardless of initial prejudice. Facilitators and co-ordinators are more likely to suffer from mistaken social consensus.

Sometimes membership of some other grouping is sufficient qualification for opinion-leadership based on expertise. Katz and Lazarsfeld (1955) have demonstrated that young girls tend to be opinion-leaders, where fashions are concerned, for women of other ages. The other women have sense enough not to consider them opinion-leaders in other spheres of life, where they might be less reliable. Their opinion-leadership is restricted to the field in which they are known experts. This excellent discrimination of function, the following pages will show, is not everywhere equally well maintained.

Opinion-leadership may also rest primarily on the expression of views rather than on factual expertise. Members who specialize in giving their views need to be analysed rather carefully because the nature of the values they introduce will affect their reception by the group. The values implied in their views may be the values of the group. This will be so if that member is a sociometric star. It is the star's good fortune to exemplify to an outstanding degree those values which the members have in common. His popularity is independent of any other function, such as expertise, which he may bring to the group—what he says and does seems of necessity right to the others. If he is a view-giver, his views will be treated as proposals and given support.

Stars are opinion-leaders because they are popular. Their privileged position provides a second reason. Everybody likes to talk to them: they are therefore also likely to be better informed than other members.

Sometimes an opinion-leader is an unusually powerful person. Members of groups are often representative of outside bodies, which are thus able to exert their influence on group-decisions. Some outside bodies may by common consensus be regarded as more important than others, so that a man who comes from an important group may be treated as an opinion-leader by those who come from less distinguished circles. When he gives his views, he is likely to receive agreement. It is unfortunately true that he may gain support even when his views are not relevant to his expertise. For instance, in some groups the views of a university lecturer or a high-ranking industrial executive on almost anything are regarded as authoritative. Although in general this may be deplored, there are some reasons why, in particular instances, the views of this kind of opinion-leader should carry some weight.

First, a man who is a member of many groups, even if he is not very clever or important, will gain more information and more experience than is available to a man with fewer contacts. If, in addition, his contacts are among influential groups, he will have access to information which members might not have been able to obtain in any other way. The more exclusive the group, the more difficult it is to extract information. (The same reasoning led us to argue in the previous chapter that those higher up in an organization have access to more information than those below.) In this sense, the weighty members play a directly useful role as experts of a particular kind: 'importers of inaccessible information'. There is evidence that leading members of informal as well as of formal groups have contacts with more important and socially remote groups than other members have. The prestige that attaches to hobnobbing with the great is an encouragement to the continued performance of this function.

Second, members who have made a number of correct recommendations in the past create for themselves what Barnard has called a 'margin of trust'. When they then express their views on a subject, their previous good judgment will enable them to carry the day, whether the members appreciate their reasons or not. This is of course especially true when members cannot verify all the relevant considerations for themselves, but have to rely on 'what everybody says': on social reality and not on proven facts. And this is in turn especially likely if some information is thought to have been confidentially given them by otherwise inaccessible groups. Those members who are thought to be most in touch and best qualified to make guesses become opinion-leaders.

There are also view-givers who are not opinion-leaders. The values they wish to insist on are not considered important by the group. The facts they bring forward are deemed less worthy of notice. Rightly or wrongly, they cannot receive support. Taylor was such a one in the education-grant episode in chapter 4, and chapter 11 gives other examples. View-givers whose values are not shared are in an uncomfortable position. If they continue to hold their views, they will be given the treatment for deviants described in chapter 6. Their existence points to the importance of analysing roles not only in terms of the contribution intended but also in terms of the response actually elicited, of analysing the interaction-matrix not only in terms of the rows but also in terms of the columns.

There will at times also be members who specialize in an agreement-role. Obviously they are not likely to be indiscriminate: they will support someone in the group who is for them an opinion-leader. These can be called supporters, dependent on some other member of the group. They can be easily discerned from an interaction-matrix because their agreement is always directed towards the same recipient. That they expect to gain from this service is suggested by the rude names that other members have invented for those who play this particular role.

There is some evidence that people who are not considered influential tend to be supporters of this kind. They like the influential members, seek to interact with them, and, rather pathetically, are prone to overestimating the extent to which the influential members like them. They also tend to overestimate the quality of the performance of the influential members. It is interesting to note that the influentials share this over-estimation of their powers. Thus, the whole group may be engaged in a common illusion, which is, to them, social reality.

In many experimental groups made up of randomly selected members, or presumably in any group in which members do not know each other very well and are inexperienced, the sheer talkatives tend to be influential in this way. Bales had found that the most talkative members are often credited by the others as having done most towards a solution of a problem, and Riecken tried to see how far this judgment was correct. His findings are most interesting. The talkative members are perceived as contributing more, and find it easier to get their solution accepted. It seems that the ability to gain the other members' attention is the significant variable here, not the ability to reason or lucidity or intelligence or persuasiveness. When the less talkative produce a solution which is accepted, they are often not perceived as having made the crucial contribution.

It is not difficult to see that an element of bluff may play a large part in imposing leadership on the group when personality-variables play a major part in the emergence of leaders. Whether a leader remains a leader, however, will depend on the contribution he can make to the task and to the survival of the group. To that extent, leadership must always remain a situational and not a personal variable. Kirscht, among others, supports this view. In his groups, as long as the members were unfamiliar to each other, the talkatives were selected as leaders. Later on, however, those who contributed most to the task were generally recognized and emerged into leadership. In the long run, performance rather than promise is bound to tell. Nevertheless, it is best to be cautious and to remember that the ability to secure agreement may be related to ability in problem-solution only in special cases. The kind of special case in which this is likely to be true will be discussed now and in the two subsequent chapters.

Except for certain considerations raised in the previous chapter, it has so far been assumed that members participate in the group because, sharing certain values, they find that a certain task needs to be undertaken and, more or less spontaneously, they find themselves co-operating in its performance. There is an important type of situation, however, in which this is not necessarily the case. The typical situation in which a group co-operates in the performance of a task which it has not chosen in accordance with its own values is the formal organization, such as a Civil Service Department, an industrial firm, or a social work agency. In this situation, the values of the organization have priority over the values of the individual.

Organizations exist for a purpose to which the members

and their satisfactions are secondary. The members can remain within the organization only by virtue of their contribution to the organization's goals. In return for the time and effort which members might otherwise have spent on activities they prefer, the organization offers inducements of money, prestige, and other satisfactions as reward.

Organizations not only set the goals, but must also impose restrictions on the ways in which the members may carry out the tasks leading to the goal. For members may differ in the way they want to work. They cannot be relied upon to work spontaneously in concord, for it is not now the members' own shared preferences which determine behaviour. Therefore the organization must make special arrangements to ensure co-operation. A co-operative group has been defined by Deutsch as a group in which a member, in the pursuit of his own ends, helps, or at least does not hinder, the other members in the pursuit of their ends. An organization has to ensure that members and groups, each occupied in some aspect of the task, do not make it impossible for other members or groups to function efficiently and effectively.

According to Simon, formal organizations share certain characteristics which, it will be seen, surmount to some extent the problem of ensuring co-operation where it does not flourish naturally.

First of all, an organization trains and indoctrinates its members. This includes not only the acquisition of the skills and techniques necessary to the new member, but also that development of common attitudes which we have already noted so often to be essential to satisfactory group membership. In this way the organization reduces the need for formal controls and sanctions, for the trained and indoctrinated member will wish to act in accordance with the ideas he has now internalized. Since other members have been through the same mill, a certain social consensus is thus created and this will make co-operation easier. It will be appreciated that there are advantages to such indoctrination, but moral dangers also.

Secondly, an organization has standard practices and a

division of labour. Each member has a position in the structure, which is such that his relationship to others and to the
performance of the work is defined. Co-operation in foresee-
able circumstances is thereby ensured, in so far as members
confine themselves to the formal structure. We have seen in
the previous chapter that they do not necessarily do so.

Thirdly, organizations have a hierarchical structure for
the transmission of information and decisions. The exact flow
of these is defined by the standard practices and the division
of labour, in so far as can be foreseen, that is, in wide terms
only. A position in this hierarchy places a man under authority. 'Of all modes of influence, authority is the one that chiefly
distinguishes the behaviour of individuals as participants in
organizations from their behaviour outside.' In practice this
means that 'the individual sets himself a general rule which
permits the communicated decision of another to guide his
own choices without deliberation as to the expedience of the
premises [on which these choices were built]'. In this phrase
the problem of securing agreement to a proposal is defined
away for members occupying a position in a formal hierarchy.

The problem is of course only defined away. Several
practical considerations remain to be dealt with. First, there
is the question of maintaining the morale of subordinates
whose reaction to a proposed line of action an appointed
leader cannot always take into account. This is dealt with more
fully in the chapter on morale. As it happens, role-expecta-
tions in our culture are such that, in larger formal groups,
people expect leaders to behave in a more autocratic way, and
themselves to participate less actively in making decisions.
Psychologically, these attitudes would be related to the kind
of 'supporter-behaviour' which was discussed earlier in this
chapter.

Secondly, there is the question of differences in quality.
There are good bosses and bad. Hemphill, who also provides
some of the evidence on which the previous paragraph is
based, finds that the superior appointed leaders in larger
groups differed from the mediocre on a number of criteria: they
worked harder and longer; they tended not to reverse decisions

once made; they tended to co-ordinate different jobs; they tended to delegate authority 'wisely'; they tended to know the technical details of the job; they tended to know the job; they tended to try and do a good job.

This rather impressionistically-worded list fits in very nicely with our own theoretical scheme: the functions of a good appointed leader are functions which must anyhow be performed in the group but which in the case of smaller leaderless groups may be distributed among a number of members, *plus* the functions of delegation and co-ordination which grow in importance with the size of the group. In formally appointed groups these functions are all expected to reside in the formally appointed leader.

For this reason it is easier for an appointed leader to be a good boss when the formal structure, as defined in chapter 7, coincides with the rational-ideal. The only rational-ideal functions which have to be fulfilled for good performance of the task are information-giving and collecting, facilitation, co-ordination, and morale-maintenance. A good boss is therefore one whose contribution will be based on more information, and often on more inaccessible information, than his subordinates can contribute. As a good facilitator he will make it possible for his subordinates to contribute according to their especial expertise. He will ensure that his subordinates are clear about the requirements of the task by giving the information necessary to an understanding of the task's requirements. His views, which will determine how the task is to be performed by his subordinates, will take into consideration all the information and all the values relevant to the task. How this relates to morale will be shown in the next chapter.

Finally, like influential members in other groups, the appointed leader can secure agreement because he can distribute rewards. In a formal organization continued membership, promotion, and a rise in salary are among the rewards which he can dispense. A good boss is one from whom these rewards can be secured by agreeing with the task-requirements rather than with the boss at his more self-expressive. This ability to reward and promote puts the appointed leader in a category rather different from that of the elected leader, for it means that he is seen as responsible for the differences in appointed status among his subordinates. Members will react to him in ways which are partly determined by their judgment of the justice of the existing differences. Low-status members who feel that they are justly in their lowly position, and that others are justly in their higher, will be satisfied. So, by and large, will the low-status members who can count on the possibility of promotion, and high-status members who have arrived there. But at any level, members who feel they have been unjustly disadvantaged will react with hostility, withdrawal (lack of interest) or deviance. One frequent special case of this kind occurs when subordinates feel they are better at their job than the appointed leader is at his. The two examples in chapter 7 provided a good illustration of this. The kind of measures the appointed leader can take to avoid this situation will be discussed in the next two chapters.

The following example, from a student's essay, shows the interweaving of types of influence and authority in the complexities of an actual organization at work.

Influential members and their influence

There is a mission hospital which is under the jurisdiction of the diocese in which it is situated. It is a training hospital for African nurses, and these students are in the charge of African staff nurses, under European sisters, under a European Matron and Medical Superintendent. The hospital is run by a Board on which are represented the larger bodies which are concerned with the hospital, i.e. the diocese, the mission district, the Provincial Health Department. Other members are co-opted to the Board. Thus, if we consider first the Board alone, it is a group of people with a leader imposed on them—for the Chairman is the Bishop or his representative. In meetings, however, the chairman is a 'democratic' leader. It is important that the bodies represented on the Board should work in harmony, and the chairman knows that to be an effective group there must be friendly co-operation. Consequently it is a group where interaction is fairly uncontrolled and although the chairman is in general control, leadership-initiative passes from one member to the other; for example, it is the Priest-in-charge of the mission who contributes most towards the solution of problems concerning the African neighbouring villages, the expert architect who takes the initiative in solving problems of drainage, and the Matron who makes suggestions on the outlay of a sum of money donated with the proviso that it be spent on equipment for the Maternity Ward. It is fairly obvious that this is the most appropriate kind of leadership in these circumstances: full use is made of experts and cordial relations are maintained. No risk is run of offending local Africans by uninformed action, of precipitating an outbreak of typhus because the drainage is inadequate, or of landing the Maternity section with a superfluity of cots for babies and insufficient beds for mothers!

If one examines another group in the general complex, that consisting of Matron and nursing staff, the situation is less 'democratic'. Matron will inform a certain group of nurses that they will have anatomy lectures at a certain time from Sister Tutor; she does not ask them to consider what subjects they should study, and who ought to teach them, or ask them to fix a time. From the nurses' point of view the leadership is arbitrary. From the point of view of Sister Tutor and Doctor, the lecture time-table is doubtless less arbitrary: there will have been discussions before it was fixed. It seems then that in a larger organization with a hierarchical structure, some subgroups are necessarily subject to autocratic leadership, for the simple reason that it would be too absurdly impractical to run a large institution in any other way. A wise leader will doubtless temper the apparent arbitrariness of orders with an explanation, i.e. 'I have assigned this hour for this lecture because Sister Tutor has to attend a meeting with a visiting specialist at the other time. . . .'

BIBLIOGRAPHY

Members' reactions to high-status or talkative members

Norfleet B., 'Interpersonal and group productivity', *J. Social Issues* IV (1948).

Thibaut J., 'An experimental study of the cohesiveness of under-privileged groups', op. cit.

Kelley H. H., 'Communication in experimentally created hierarchies' (1951), in Cartwright and Zander, op. cit., ch. 30.

Harvey O. J., 'Status relations in informal groups', *Amer. Sociol. Review* XVIII (1953).

Thibaut J. and Riecken H. W., 'Authoritarianism, status and the communication of aggression', *Human Relations* VIII (1955).

Hurwitz J. I. *et al* (1956), 'Some effects of power on the relations among group members' (1956), in Cartwright and Zander, op. cit., ch. 30.

Klein J., *The Study of Groups*, op. cit., chs. 3–5

Cohen A. R., 'Upward communication in experimentally created hierarchies', *Human Relations* XI (1958).

Patchen M., 'The effect of reference group standards on job satisfaction', *Human Relations* XI (1958).

Riecken H. W., 'The effect of talkativeness and ability to influence group solutions of problems', *Sociometry* XXI (1958).

Mussen P. H. and Porter G. W., 'Personal motivations and self-conceptions associated with effectiveness and ineffectiveness in emergent groups', *J. Abnormal and Social Psych.* LIV (1959).

Descriptions of formal organizations

Devons E., *Planning in Wartime* (Cambridge U.P., 1950).

Jaques E., *The Changing Culture of a Factory* (Tavistock Publications, London, 1951).

Rice A. K., *Productivity and Social Organization: the Ahmedabad Experiment* (Tavistock Publications, London, 1958).

The analysis of formal organizations

Barnard C. I., *The Functions of the Executive* (Harvard U.P., Cambridge, Mass., 1938).

Simon H. A., *Administrative Behaviour* (Macmillan, London, 1947).

Trecker H. B., *Group Process in Administration* (Woman's Press, New York, 1953).

Weiss R. S., *Processes of Organization* (Michigan U.P., New York, 1956).

March J. G. and Simon H. A., *Organizations* (Wiley, New York, 1958).

Consult also the *Journal of Social Issues* (1951 and 1956). Nos. VII, 3 and XII, 2 are devoted to 'Human relations research in large organizations'.

Differences between appointed and emergent or elected leaders

Stogdill R. M., 'Personal factors associated with leadership', *J. Psych.* XXV (1943).

Stogdill R. M., 'Leadership, membership and organization' (1950), in Cartwright and Zander, op. cit., ch. 4.

Hemphill J. K., 'Relations between size of group and the behaviour of superior leaders', *J. Social Psych.* XXXII (1950).

Carter L. *et al.*, 'The behaviour of leaders and other group members' (1951), in Cartwright and Zander, op. cit., ch. 37.

Pelz D. C., 'Leadership within a hierarchical organization', *J. Social Issues* III (1951).

Chowdry K. and Newcomb T. M., 'The relative abilities of leaders and non-leaders to estimate opinions in their own groups', Hare, Borgatta and Bales, op. cit.

Berkovitz L., 'Sharing leadership in small decision-making groups', *J. Abnormal and Social Psych.* XLVIII (1953).

Sanford F. H., 'Leadership identification and acceptance', Guetzkow (ed.), *Groups, Leadership and Men* (Carnegie Press, Pittsburgh, 1954).

Borgatta E. F., Couch A. S. and Bales R. F., 'Some findings relevant to the great-man theory of leadership', Hare, Borgatta and Bales, op. cit.

Carter L., 'Some research on leadership in small groups', Guetzkowed, *Groups, Leadership and Men*, op. cit.

Adams S., 'Social climate and productivity in small military groups', *Amer. Sociol. Review* XIX (1954).

Katz E. *et al.*, 'Leadership stability and social change', *Sociometry* XX (1957).

Kirscht L. P., Lodahl T. M. and Haire M., 'Some factors in the selection of leaders by members of small groups', *J. Abnormal and Social Psych.* LVIII (1959).

9

STRUCTURE, FUNCTION, AND MORALE

For good morale there must be sufficient resources to permit the performance of the task; all members should have access to these resources and all should be able to contribute to them; the members should share the values which are furthered by the performance of the task; they should be clear how the resources can be used to further the task. In these circumstances a good division of function is likely to come about: the members will recognize the expert; they will themselves become more expert. The sociometric star can lead a group when there is no task or no attractive task; he may lose his popularity if either he, or the members without him, become deeply involved in a task. The expert can lead a group deeply involved in the task, if the group recognize his expertise. A leaderless group will be successful only when all members are experts and all know it; conversely, when all members are experts and all know it, they will work best as a leaderless group.

WE WILL now examine the relationship between the functions of members on the one hand and their morale on the other. Many attempts have been made to list the conditions making for high morale. Such lists illuminate the concept of morale, but they are too imprecise for practical purposes. The same criticisms apply to them as applied to the observation-schedules in chapter 2. The items sometimes overlap and one consideration listed may seem to conflict with another. The items are not wrong, but it is difficult to see why and how they fit together. They are not incorporated in a more general theoretical framework. This we are now ready to attempt.

We may begin with a brief operational definition: morale will be high in a group which is doing well both in the task-related and in the expressive sphere. In chapter 3 the task of a discussion-group was defined as the fitting together of ideas into a coherent whole, acceptable to all members. It will be remembered that the group constructs its plans partly out of the information which it has at its disposal, and partly from the values of the members.

In planning, when members participate in the exchange of information, they state or restate the limits with which they have to reckon if decisions are to be acceptable on rational grounds. The implication for morale is obvious: all task-related functions must be adequately performed. A detailed consideration of what this means for morale—to expert, facilitator, and co-ordinator—must be postponed until later in the chapter.

Plans are made to further certain ends, or valued goals. Ends, as well as means, affect a group's morale. For they limit the extent to which members are willing to be associated with an agreement or a decision. The lower limit is, that no part of the task should be performed in such a way as to outrage the values held by any individual member. The upper limit is, that all members should feel deeply committed to the values which the task is intended to further. Therefore it is important, first, that the members should be aware of the value-implications in whatever proposals are being made, and second, that they should have the opportunity to react, participating by agreement or disagreement, to the proposals that are made. (It goes without saying that they should be able to put forward views and proposals of their own as one form of reaction.) If any of these conditions is violated, the neglected member will feel that the decision is not morally binding for him. His morale will suffer because he may with reason feel that those who impose decisions upon him are prepared to do without his consent; and the group's morale will suffer if the outraged member becomes disloyal, skimps his work, or in other ways eludes the control that would otherwise be exerted by his personal commitment to the commonly agreed task.

Finally among these preliminary considerations, it should be remembered that a certain amount of expressive interaction is necessary for good morale. First, these informal exchanges tend to have the effect of making the members more like-minded. They produce a consensus of values and views, so that there will be fewer occasions for disagreements about ends and means. Certain tasks and certain ways of task-performance will come to seem the obviously right ones. Secondly, if people like each other, they will want to express that liking in informal interaction. If they have no opportunity of doing this, they may feel that the task is a hindrance to their self-expression. This will affect their performance of the task, and this will in turn feed back to a further lowering of morale.

The balance between expressive and task-related behaviour is a tricky one to achieve. If there is too much good-fellowship, it may lead later to dissatisfaction because the work has been piling up to unmanageable proportions. On the other hand, an excess of devotion to the task may defeat its own object, since it will reduce for some members the pleasure of belonging to this particular group with these particular members.

Three experimental studies may form the starting-point for a more practical consideration of the participation of leaders and members in a group, and its relation to morale. The first concerns a sociometric study of relationships in two U.S. naval air squadrons:

> Both squadrons were made up of a commanding officer, an executive officer, and 17 flying personnel . . . The 17 men in each squadron were asked to state anonymously their personal preferences as to men they knew (inside the squadron or out of it) whom they would like to have fly beside them. They were also asked to name men they would not like to have fly beside them. The results for each squadron were plotted in a sociogram (overleaf). A solid line with arrow indicates a choice, a dotted line a rejection. Persons named outside the squadron are shown outside the enclosing square.

In Squadron A it is notable that the commanding officer (CO) was named favourably by eight men and the executive officer (XO) by six. In Squadron B, in sharp contrast, the CO was named by no one, either positively

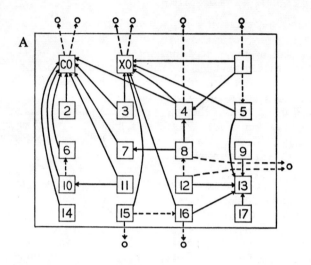

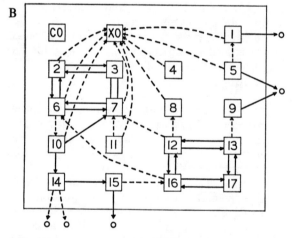

or negatively, and the XO received no favourable mentions and nine rejections. On this evidence alone . . . it is easy to recognize the superiority of morale of Squadron A over Squadron B.

There are other equally revealing indications. In Squadron B we see the existence of two subgroups or cliques within the whole—one made up of individuals 2, 3, 6, and 7; the other of 12, 13, 16, and 17 . . . each individual being chosen and choosing in return. No member of either of these cliques chose anyone outside the tight little group. Squadron A, in contrast, contains no apparent segregated subgroups of this sort . . .

A third interesting indication of the difference in morale of the two groups is seen in the relative incidence of favourable and unfavourable mention outside the squadron itself. In Squadron A there were no choices of men outside the squadron and ten rejections; in Squadron B the proportions were reversed, there being four choices outside and only two rejections.[1]

This study has several lessons to teach. First, if morale and co-operation with friends are so closely associated, it is obviously worth while, other things being equal, to find out which members are friendly with each other when it is necessary to divide the group into subgroups in clubs, working parties, and the like. Secondly, in the squadron with high morale, the appointed leaders are also the most popular members of the group. This is always significant of high morale, and is as a rule only possible in groups where all members are able to recognize skill and where the appointed leaders are also the most skilled.

A second study provides a warning at this juncture. Once friends have found themselves a task, friendship is no longer enough. They will want to do well at their chosen work. Otherwise they will sit around depressing each other. T. T. Paterson (1955) studied some British R.A.F. units with low morale. These units felt dissatisfied because they were not sufficiently often in contact with the enemy. The members were highly skilled, liked their leaders and each other, disliked

[1] From Krech D. and Crutchfield D., *Theory and Problems in Social Psychology* (McGraw-Hill, New York, 1948), reporting on an unpublished study by J. G. Jenkins.

outside groups, but morale was low, for they did badly in the task-related area: for instance, they had many flying accidents. Paterson had the ingenuity to reorganize their perceptions so that they came to feel that the force of gravity and the bad weather were part of the task against which they must test themselves. He was successful in bringing down the accident rate. In bringing about this change in perception—this change, one might say, in their point of view—he approached the leaders first: those in the group who were both highly skilled and very popular. When they responded, the solidary group that had performed badly became a solidary group that did its task well: this is how high morale may be defined.

A third study shows how the leader of a group can encourage or inhibit a 'group-atmosphere' which affects the development of involvement in the task, of membership-participation in the task and of general friendliness in the group, by encouraging or inhibiting free interaction between the members.

Leadership in two new boys' clubs differed in the following respects:

Group A	*Group B*
1. The leader decided what task the group should perform.	1. The group discussed a variety of possible tasks and chose one. The leader encouraged them and gave information when needed.
2. The leader did not tell the members how they would set about the task, but told them what to do, one step at a time, so that they could only guess why they were doing their particular job. They did not know what it led to or why it was the best thing to do in the circumstances.	2. The leader explained the general steps that would need to be taken at the first meeting. Where technical advice was needed, the leader tried to point out two or three alternative procedures from which choice would be made.

3. The leader distributed the tasks among the members and decided who should work with whom.

3. The members were free to work with whom they chose, and the division of tasks was left to the members.

4. The leader was 'personal' in his praise and criticism of the work of each member without giving objective reasons. He remained aloof from active group participation except when demonstrating.

4. The leader was 'objective' or 'factminded' in his praise and criticism and tried to be a regular group member in spirit without doing too much of the actual work.

The consequences of these two leadership techniques are those one would expect. It was found after the task was finished that members of group A did not care for the products of their work (puppets and small statues). They jumped on them and destroyed them in a kind of riot. Members of group B proudly took their achievements home. Group A were against the continuation of the group with a new task, whereas the others wanted to go on. During the meetings, members of group B had been more absorbed in their tasks. They continued working when the leader was out of the room, while group A stopped at once and engaged in rough horse-play. Members of group B were co-operative and relaxed, and stood up well to criticism; those of group A were either very apathetic and withdrawn or very aggressive, and criticism quite disrupted them. Indeed, two members of the latter group left before the end of the series of meetings, because they had been made butts and scapegoats by the others.

The reasons for these differences are not far to seek. Clearly, much more interaction between the members took place in group B than in group A, where they had constantly to consult the leader before they could get on with their work. When interaction is mainly between leader and individual member, and the interaction between individual members is controlled almost entirely by the leader, there is just not enough informal contact between the members to generate liking. Moreover, even boys have values and preferences which they desire to express. Normally, these would find expression in the way the resources of the group are utilized for the achievement of a common goal. (In an adult group these resources tend to be ideas—here they are material, but that does not alter the argument.) If the leader sets the goal, it may not be one desired by the members. If only the leader knows the goal, the others cannot co-operate with him in attaining it, even if they wanted to. If the leader is also the distributor of the materials used to attain the goal, the members cannot choose the function that they prefer to perform or know themselves to be expert in. A proper distribution of function is also prevented by the leader's insistence on submissive obedience. If no proper division of function can emerge, members may seek to retain their self-respect through scapegoating or aggression.

We may now draw some general conclusions on the functions of members and the nature of morale, derived from the points considered in this and the previous chapters.

Stars. The group may be one in which members share a number of the values important to all. It may be a group of friends who just like to be together and who do not think of themselves as having a task to perform. They will not need a leader. One of the members is likely to exemplify the common values of the group more closely than the others do—he will be a star. In so far as the group's short-term plans and activities need to be directed, he will do it in an informal sort of way.

Where there is no task, there need be no appointed leader to give orders. If it should become necessary that someone represent the group, say on a higher-level committee, there is no reason why the most popular and generally admired and trusted member should not be invited. Such a member may be identified either by voting or from a sociometric study. He will also be the best channel through which persuasion to change can travel, for if he can be convinced, the others will follow him, as he is already a model for them in other ways.

Similarly where the group does have a task to perform in which the members are not particularly involved, i.e. which they do not really value, the star will be the best bet as the leader. If he can be made to feel responsible for the task, the others will follow him; if he is against the task, the others will also feel unwilling. In many situations, authority has on occasion to be delegated. A popular member has more chance of exerting 'informal prestige' and 'unsanctioned authority' on such occasions than other members have, although it is obviously not advisable to select the chairmen of sub-committees by sociogram!

Experts. The group may be one in which the members share a number of the values important to them all, and which desires to further these values in action. That is, the group values the task which it has chosen to perform. When deeply involved members lack the knowledge necessary to perform the task, or lack the necessary experts, there will obviously be a fall in morale.

Deeply involved members will follow whoever knows most about the task. They will not mind whether their leader is appointed or elected, provided they can recognize his expertise. If the leader is appointed, there will be a fall in morale if he is not the expert or if he does not allow the recognized expert scope and status.

Facilitators. Deeply involved members will want to contribute. Otherwise they will feel that they are wasting their time in the group, or that their usefulness is being ignored. Morale will suffer accordingly. Every member who wants to contribute should be given the opportunity to do so.

Co-ordinators. Deeply involved members may be handicapped because they do not know how to set about their chosen task. The task may have been badly defined, and the role-structure may then be inappropriate to good performance. One instance of this is particularly relevant. A complex task is not often a single-step one, but tends to consist of a sequence of problems, each having to be solved before the next can be attempted. The members may be so preoccupied with their ultimate goal that they are too impatient to consider the necessary steps on the road towards it. And the first essential step is likely to be: to work out a procedure which allows the problems to be dealt with one by one. The frustrating feeling of 'not getting any forrader' can often be traced to a mistaken idea of the nature of the task: the preliminaries are seen as wrong ends rather than as necessary means. This is as true in a discussion-group or a committee as it is in manual tasks. An organizational expert or co-ordinator is therefore required to help the members to consider the steps whereby they should proceed and the role-structure which would be best in the circumstances. Provided he does this, it makes no difference whether he is the appointed leader or a member playing a self-appointed role. This means, incidentally, that an appointed leader should be slow to break up the naturally-evolved structure of the group. However, it can also happen that the group evolves a rigid structure which gradually or suddenly becomes inappropriate to its circumstances. The effects of this may now be examined.

Status-struggles and status-congruence. In informal groups, the star, who exemplifies the values of the group, is likely to play an important part in defining what task the group shall take on. Having done this he may find himself in a curious position, for a star is not necessarily an expert, and the group will now be requiring an expert. Indeed, there is some evidence that leadership in expressive relationships and leadership in task-related activities tend to be taken on by different people. Slater suggests a reason why this may be so. The popular member needs to be liked; consequently he adjusts himself to the needs of the group. The man of ideas is too interested in the task to take so much notice of the response of others; he expects the group to adjust itself to him. Any man who does this obviously risks the loss of his popularity. Slater also suggests that extreme separation of these two types of leadership is characteristic of groups with low morale. Other evidence indicates that such a split is more likely in the early stages of a group's development.

When the group's circumstances change markedly, therefore, there may be a struggle for leadership. Divided leadership is not likely to be conducive to good morale in the group. During that struggle the unwise star who insists on retaining his ascendancy may lose sociometric standing and the expert will almost certainly gain in popularity.

When the struggle is over, the task-structure and the sociometric structure of the group may be congruent again, in which case morale will be high. When this stage is reached, there may be a slight decline in the quality of task-performance.

The reason for this slight decline may be found in the changing behaviour of the expert during his struggle upward. Several studies confirm the common-sense view that emergent leaders are more pushing than those who have arrived. It is not difficult to conceive of circumstances in which the extra push they exert during their upward climb outweighs the ill effects of the status-struggle. Once they have arrived, they need not and do not push quite so hard. They become less controlling and they may delegate some of these controlling functions to their supporters or seconds-in-command, while they set about achieving sociometric status. (The group will, of course, only put up with the more pushing and autocratic behaviour of the emergent leader if they are very anxious to see the task performed, if the emergent leader can really help them and if they can recognize his expertise.)

The advantages of general participation. Participation reduces redundancy. General participation is a characteristic of the co-operative group. This is a logical tautology if, after Deutsch, a co-operative group is defined as one in which the members are interdependent in such a way that they all share the same goal and that each member's progress towards the goal helps the other members in their progress. In a co-operative situation X perceives himself as nearer his goal as a consequence of Y's action. He will therefore be less likely to repeat a contribution already made by Y: there will be less redundant activity.

Participation increases the members' satisfaction with each other. X will be pleased with Y's contribution and reward it, either by friendly expressive behaviour or by a further task-related contribution of his own, which will, incidentally, also help Y (by definition). There will, then, be mutual encouragement among the members, a greater helpfulness, more emotional involvement, and often a better division of labour.

Participation increases substitutability. Deutsch argues that in a co-operative group the members are often better able, and certainly more willing, to do each other's work. They can and do substitute for one another at a pinch. This is not only convenient for good task-performance. Many industrial studies give evidence that the variety of work made possible by such a voluntarily chosen arrangement is considered rewarding and keeps morale high.

Participation relieves the load of work on the leader, at least in the long run. It is safe to say that when the members have too much leisure, the leader has too much work. Neither of these conditions is conducive to high morale. Participation relieves the leader's work-load because it trains the members to see what needs doing.

Participation trains the members to recognize expertise. It may happen that the members, though anxious to see the task performed, do not know enough about it to recognize the expert and to allow him to lead. He may, for instance, be seen as obstructive because he reminds the group of inconvenient facts. This may lead to a typical status-struggle: the expert's leadership will be challenged and the star may be exploited as a stick to beat him with. This is a very unsatisfactory condition, because the group needs the expert's help in performing the task: morale will sink, not only because of the warfare but also because the task is not being performed as well as it might be.

In the course of co-operating, the members gain first-hand insight into the difficulties and the possible solutions of the problem that faces the group. As members work at their task, they become experts at their share of it. As members are getting trained in the performance of tasks they will gain insight into the competence of other members of the group. They will recognize the expert as qualified to give the orders, because they recognize that he is good at his job. Of course, this may prove a two-edged weapon, for they may be contemptuous if they find the expert is no good. This is sometimes hard for the insecure leader to accept. However, unless he recognizes their expertise in his turn, not only will he lose information about the task, but, when orders are given which the members believe are not the best in the circumstances, morale will be lowered.

Participation relieves the problem of control. If everyone knows what the task requires, generally speaking the pattern of interaction will not be 'orders from the top, obedience at the lower levels', but 'orders from the top based on information from all ranks'. Since orders in the latter case are based on information, it is hardly possible for them to be unintelligible, and they will not be felt as arbitrary commands but as common-sense advice.

It should be clear that where members share the relevant facts and values, most information implies a proposal. The members can see how the information excludes some kinds of decision that might otherwise have been made. Subjectively, in these circumstances, information and proposals are felt simply to be 'information and proposals'. When members do not share a frame of reference in this way, proposals made by one who has the power to enforce them are felt subjectively to be 'orders'.

The more effective groups are characterized by greater participation in problem-definition and problem-solution. This is so even when there is 'strong' leadership. If such a leader permits a wide divergence of expressed ideas and allows the group to thresh out the difficulties, he will eventually be able to gain greater acceptance for his decision (if it is right). Torrance has pointed out that a leader's tolerance of disagreement increases the range of available judgments and decreases the chances of misunderstanding. He was able to prove that this enables leaders to take greater risks than they might otherwise have taken, because they can know beforehand whether the group will back them.

There is good empirical and theoretical support for the view that, especially when the problems to be solved are complicated and require a number of different skills, a very varied group has a better chance of a good solution than a very homogeneous group; but full use can only be made of all these different types of skill if general participation can be secured. This is the responsibility of the facilitator. The next chapter begins with a discussion of the techniques he has at his disposal for the exercise of this responsibility.

BIBLIOGRAPHY

Lists of desiderata for morale

Watson G., 'Five factors in morale', in his book *Civilian Morale* (Reynal and Hitchcock, New York, 1942).

Allport G. W., 'The nature of democratic morale', Watson (ed.), *Civilian Morale*, op. cit.

Cartwright D. and Zander A., *Group Dynamics*, op. cit., ch. 22.

Group atmospheres

Lippitt R., 'An experimental study of the effect of democratic and authoritarian group atmospheres', *University of Iowa Studies in Child Welfare* XVI (1940).

White R. and Lippitt R., 'Leader behaviour and member reaction in three social climates' (1956), in Cartwright and Zander, op. cit., ch. 40.

Stars, experts, facilitators and co-ordinators

Thibaut J., 'An experimental study of the cohesiveness of under-privileged groups', op. cit.

Bass B. M. *et al.*, 'Interacting effects of control, motivation, group practice and problem difficulty on attempted leadership', *J. Abnormal and Social Psych.* LVI (1958).

Kelley H. H., 'Communication in experimentally created hier-archies', op. cit.

Borg W. R., 'The behaviour of emergent and designated leaders in situational tests', *Sociometry* XX (1957).

Horwitz M., 'The recall of interrupted group tasks: an experimental study of individual motivation in relation to group goals', *Human Relations* VI (1953) and abridged in Cartwright and Zander, op. cit.

Klein J., *The Study of Groups*, op. cit., chs. 1–2.

McCurdy H. G. and Lambert V. E., 'The efficiency of small groups in the solution of problems requiring genuine co-operation', *J. Personality* XX (1952).

McCurdy H. G. and Eber H. W., 'Democratic *v.* authoritarian: a further investigation into group problem-solving', *J. Personality* XXI (1953).

Status struggles and status congruence

Hollander E. P. and Webb W. B., 'Leadership, followership and friendship: an analysis of peer nominations', *J. Abnormal and Social Psych.* L (1955).

Slater P. E., 'Role-differentiation in small groups', Hare, Borgatta and Bales, op. cit.

Heinicke C. and Bales R. F., 'Developmental trends in the structure of small groups', op. cit.

Adams S., 'Status congruency as a variable in small group performance', *Social Forces* XXXII (1953).

Carter L. *et al.*, 'The behaviour of leaders and other group members', op. cit.

Carter L., 'Leadership and small group behaviour', Sherif and Wilson (ed.), *Group Relations at the Cross Roads* (Harper, New York, 1953).

Gross N., Martin W. E. and Darley J. G., 'Studies of group behaviour'. *J. Abnormal and Social Psych.* XLVIII (1953).

Co-operation and competition

Deutsch M., 'The effects of co-operation and competition upon group process', op. cit.

Israel J., *Self-evaluation and Rejection in Groups*, op. cit.

Rice A. K., *Productivity and Social Organization: the Ahmedabad Experiment*, op. cit.

Thomas E. J., 'Effects of facilitative role interdependence on group functioning', *Human Relations* X (1957).

Advantages of general participation

Hare A. P., 'Interaction and consensus in different-sized groups' (1942), in Cartwright and Zander, op. cit., ch. 34.

Follett M. P., *Freedom and Co-ordination* (Management Publ. Trust, London, 1949).

Preston M. G. and Heintz R. K., 'Effects of participatory and supervisory leadership on group judgement' (1949), in Cartwright and Zander, op. cit., ch. 37.

Ichheiser G., 'Misunderstandings in human relations', *Amer. J. Sociol.* LV (1949–50).

Fouriezos N. T., Hutt M. L. and Guetzkow H., 'Self-oriented needs in discussion groups', *J. Abnormal and Social Psych.* XLV (1950) and abridged in Cartwright and Zander, op. cit.

Bovard E. W., 'Group structure and perception' (1951), in Cartwright and Zander, op. cit., ch. 14.

Schachter S. *et al.*, 'An experimental study of cohesiveness and productivity' (1951), in Cartwright and Zander, op. cit., ch. 27.

Berkovitz L., 'Sharing leadership in small decision-making groups', op. cit.

Berkovitz L., 'Group standards, cohesiveness and productivity', *Human Relations* VII (1954).

Adams S., 'Social climate and productivity in small military groups', op. cit.

Klein J., *The Study of Groups*, op. cit., chs. 3, 6–10.

Torrance E. P., 'Group decision-making and disagreement', *Social Forces* XXXV (1956–7).

de Charmis R., 'Affiliation motivation and productivity in small groups', *J. Abnormal and Social Psych.* LV (1957).

Hoffman L. R., 'Homogeneity of member personality and its effect on group problem solving', *J. Abnormal and Social Psych.* LVIII (1959).

CHANGING IDEAS IN THEORY AND PRACTICE

Ideas confine a man to certain social groups and social groups confine a man to certain ideas. Many ideas are more easily changed by aiming at a group than by aiming at an individual. The unfreezing of ideas is the normal consequence of entering a new group; it is achieved through contact with new facts and new values. A skilled discussion-leader can create conditions favourable to the unfreezing of old ideas and commitment to new ones. This skill is a practical application of knowledge of the normal decison-making process. The techniques available for changing ideas can also be used in committee; the chairman normally plays the part of the skilled discussion-leader, but many components of his role can be taken over by other members.

THE conditions which produce an efficient and happy discussion-group need not be left to chance. The present chapter is concerned with an examination of the techniques which the members have at their disposal to secure good conditions. Normally, of course, the main responsibility for this rests on the discussion-leader or the chairman. But it has already been shown that it is more important that the necessary functions should be performed than that they should be performed by the officially appointed member. The use of these techniques is therefore open to anyone.

First, however, it may be fruitful to look again at the origin of the ideas exchanged in discussion, and in particular to stress their social nature.

If a man has a more or less integrated personality, he will have more or less consistent ideas. Some of these will go very deep, arising out of, as well as shaping, his most fundamental views of life. This tends to be true for facts as well as for more personal preferences and values.

Most of these ideas will not have been acquired by a deliberate effort of the intelligence: a man does not usually examine and sift ideas, finally giving allegiance only to those that are truest and most elevating. The ideas that form his working capital depend to a great extent on the social groups of which he is a member. In so far as ideas are shared by those with whom one is in frequent contact, they will remain unexamined and unverified. The social consensus supports them: there is no encouragement to question them. They may indeed be supported by factual evidence, but emotionally they are retained because in the group they are regarded as obvious and proper: they constitute social reality.

In addition, people who have interests in common seek each other out to talk shop. This is not only because they are useful to each other in adding to the other's stock of facts. They get on well together because they share the same values —both ideas about what pursuits are worth while and ideas that are formed and strengthened by the disciplines required to pursue these interests successfully. Consider the facts, values, and views likely to be current in a family keen on bird-watching or Bach, in a local dramatic society or tennis club, among amateur botanists or jazz enthusiasts. Members of such groups share the same kinds of knowledge and, to some extent, the same kinds of ignorance as well.

Just as shared ideas create or cement groups, so unshared ideas serve to isolate and divide. Just as we tend to seek out and like those who share our ideas, so we tend to avoid and be a little bored by those who disagree with us, who will not understand us, or whose stock of facts or values seems strange to us. We tend to feel on these occasions that the others are wrong, not merely different, and though we cannot put a finger on the argument that would convince them, we feel sure that there is such an argument somewhere. Just as group membership serves to confirm ideas when members happen to share them, so members will regard with doubt and suspicion anyone who does not share their ideas; they will feel that he is not 'one of us' if he does not see what is so self-evident to them. Unfamiliar ideas may be ignored, may not even be heard, or may provoke hostility.

The result is that ideas are difficult to alter. A man under pressure to change his ideas may be deterred by the fear of appearing odd to his friends. The advantages of changing ideas through group action rather than by changing isolated individuals are therefore clear. The individual, embedded in his group, will lose his standing in the group if he changes and they do not. If he values his group he will be anxious not to find himself in conflict, and it will be relatively more difficult to persuade him to change. Conversely, if all the members of the group can be persuaded together, the new attitude will be supported by the same social forces that had supported the previous attitude.

According to Lewin, changes of attitude in the group, as elsewhere, move through three phases:

a. an 'unfreezing' of previous attitudes,

b. a change in attitude and

c. a 'freezing' of the new attitude.

Unfreezing

Before any change is possible the inadequacy of present behaviour must be recognized. This is the 'unfreezing' process. In interaction, this may start quite informally, when one member makes a suggestion for action which seems quite obvious to him, only to find that others are unwilling to agree. The ground on which they disagree informs him of further considerations which he has to take into account, if he still wants the group to take the action he advocates. Or he may find, on entering a new group, that the grounds on which other members make decisions are quite different from those he habitually considers. In the first case he finds that he has not (or they have not) taken all the facts into account: it may be the wrong time of year, or the place may be too far away, or the necessary resources may not be available. In other words his (or their) information may be at fault. In the second case he finds that other people have preferences different from his own, and that some considerations, say kindliness, may count more for him than for them, whereas they would rather be efficient than kind. In other words, they do not share all his values. In such a case, even when he ultimately still maintains his own ranking of preferences intact, there is a period of uncertainty during which he recognizes that the decision he advocates is not the obvious and inevitable one for all.

There are, however, also many personal habits of thought and expression which have no factual or moral significance in themselves and which yet make it difficult for the group to arrive at the best possible course of action (or inaction) in the circumstances. According to Maier, who has done a good deal of work on the training of discussion-leaders, we tend to be handicapped in our thinking by being frozen in a habit of thought which has ceased to be efficient. 'If we are to influence or aid the thinking of others, this can more readily be achieved by recognizing and influencing the direction their thinking is taking.' Such recognition and influence, which is a kind of 'unfreezing', takes place naturally in a group at any time, just because nobody thinks along exactly the same lines as everyone else. On the other hand, there are ways in which the group handicaps good thinking. The most important of these handicaps is that some people, who are not necessarily less intelligent, are more diffident in putting forward their own views; also, their ability may be underestimated in a particular group so that their opinions are not listened to with the same respect or attention as are those of other more highly esteemed, but not necessarily more intelligent, members of the group.

For both these reasons it is important that someone in the group, normally the discussion-leader or chairman, plays a facilitating role, particularly when it is desired to introduce a change of outlook into a rather inward-looking group with settled views. This presents the outside expert with formidable problems. And yet such cases are more frequent than one might think. Besides the professional social scientist who accepts an assignment to smooth over or introduce a change, there are others who are technical experts in their field—Members of Parliament, engineers, youth club leaders, the clergy—who may advocate a policy which they believe to be a good one on grounds connected with their own expertise and yet find themselves in difficulties because of their lack of social skills.

Maier has written out a set of instructions for the expert who finds himself working with an unskilled group. They are reproduced in italics below, with a commentary to bring out their implications more fully and to show their relevance to the argument pursued in this book.

1. *Do not present the group with a problem but instead determine from the group whether they have a problem.* If the expert attempts to change opinions or behaviour, he must start from where the people concerned stand. They may have another problem which is so urgent to them that they hardly have attention to spare for what he is saying, and which may wrongly colour the problem he desires to present to them. It may also be noted that by this means the expert, who is often more articulate and more definite in his views than the rest of the committee, may be prevented from confusing the issue by imposing his own values on the others. Tolerance of what seems irrelevant in the early stages may avoid a lot of irrelevant discussion when the group finally gets down to brass tacks.

2. *Make a list of all suggestions so that all types of considerations are included.* No one knows beforehand which information and which values will be felt to be essential. When the time for proposals comes, it is very hard to remember everything that has been contributed. A list serves as a kind of collective memory and keeps the attention of a member on all the points that have been made, not merely on those that had an immediate appeal for him. A blackboard is ideal for this purpose, because then people can see what has gone before, and this may stimulate them to think further. If there is no blackboard, a competent secretary, who may be the expert himself, to write down all the suggestions and repeat them at intervals, is essential.

3. *Recognize all suggestions and protect individuals from the criticism of other group-members by interpreting all remarks in a favourable light.* This must be done to preserve good feeling in the group and to avoid any impression of favouritism. A really skilled leader has a chance here, in the process of repeating and interpreting members' contributions, to disentangle the fact element from the value element. It is fruitful, although not always possible, to keep several lists: one of relevant facts and one of relevant values. Explicit proposals should be separately recorded and discussion of them postponed until it is felt that information-exchange is complete.

4. *Good suggestions may be kept in the discussion by asking 'how would that work out?' etc.* In this way a man has the chance of explaining in more detail; and the more valuable ideas are given proper prominence.

5. *Do not hasten the solution by capitalizing on the first good lead or in any other way reflect your preferences.* The expert must never forget that there may be a better solution than the one he has in mind. He must be patient in accumulating all information that may conceivably be relevant to a solution of the problem. Even what he considers to be irrelevant may, for reasons he has not explored, be felt by the members to be closely connected with the problem.

6. *When the list is fairly complete, probing questions may be asked, e.g. 'how can we change things so as to combine some of these features?' etc.* This is the stage of proposal and agreement. It is at this point that the 'co-ordinator' is required. This stage should not be too quickly reached. When it comes, all members must be encouraged to participate. They must be involved in the decision-making process if they are to feel that the solution is their own.

This whole sequence is part of the 'unfreezing' process. Not only is knowledge of fact submitted openly to all concerned for criticism and correction, but a loosening-up of old habits of thought is also encouraged. The members are stimulated into looking at the problem in the round and they themselves are often astonished to find that they are abandoning trains of thought they have long taken for granted. Of course, this momentary effect will not last, another habit will soon be built up, but at this moment the opportunity presents itself to make a change.

Freezing

It is to be hoped that by these techniques someone will finally make a proposal for action and that the group will come to agreement. To what can disagreement be due? Either to the fact that some members need further information before they can be persuaded, in which case the group moves back to the unfreezing exchange of information, or else to the fact that the deviant individuals estimate the information in the light of values and preferences not shared by the group. Ultimately, nothing can be done about this latter problem—*de gustibus non est disputandum*—but it may be said in passing that only a very strong personality can stand out against group pressures, and one may ask oneself whether the deviant does not belong to some other group which has more influence on him and through which one would have to work if one sought to reach him.

If, however, agreement is reached, the information that went into that agreement will now keep the decision at once stable and flexible, knowledge of fact and value consensus contributing to the same end. The members know exactly what considerations led to the decision and are therefore capable of adjusting in an informed way to minor changes in circumstance—hence the decision will be flexible. The members would have to be strongly impressed by a new item of information before they changed again—therefore the decision will be stable. Further, stability may be maintained because in any group in which members see each other from day to day there is a constant check on whether the new plan is still being followed. It is difficult to be a backslider in such circumstances.

The line of argument pursued here derives from a very large number of studies on attitude-changes and decision-making in small groups. Coch and French used the technique for introducing changes in methods of work and payment in a sewing-machine factory, Levine and Butler in teaching foremen to assess their workers' performance correctly, Lewin in persuading American housewives in wartime to use 'offal' meats like liver, sweetbreads, and kidneys, Jaques to increase efficiency at high management level and improve inter-level understanding at a London engineering works.

The technique works, and it has from the beginning been taken for granted that the explanation of its efficacy lies in a combination of intellectual factors and emotional group pressures. Because the members of the group *participate* in the deliberations that lead up to the change and because they *participate* in encouraging and exhorting each other to maintain the new situation, it has been thought that the discussion method is responsible for these effects, which the straightforward lecture or announcement had failed to bring about. But recently Bennett has queried the too facile conclusions that have been drawn at times from the studies mentioned above. Her starting point is the following argument: 'The investigators found that a group of housewives who participated in a discussion and made a public decision by raising their hands, and were then told that there would be a follow-up study to check on what they did, were more likely to serve non-preferred meat than another group who listened to a lecture without making a decision and without being told to expect a follow-up study.'

She therefore set up an experiment in which it was possible to distinguish not only between the effects of a lecture versus those of a group discussion, but also between subjects who were induced to come to a definite decision (*either* after discussion *or* after a lecture) and subjects who were not asked to make such a decision (again either after a lecture or after discussion). In this study the action desired was that students should volunteer to be guinea-pigs in a psychological experiment that was to be held later in the week, and it was on this that the students had to make a decision. Bennett found that there was less difference in response between the groups who discussed and those who were lectured to, than between groups who were asked to decide then and there and those who were not. She concludes that *it is a deliberate commitment to a course of action, rather than the fact of discussion, that 'freezes' the new attitude.*

Clearly Bennett's study was timely and her contribution to our knowledge of group-changes very valuable. But it is important to realize, for fear of undervaluing what has been said on the subject of 'unfreezing', that generally no very deep-seated attitudes or settled habits are involved in being a guinea-pig. For Bennett's subjects, therefore, clarification of issues, insight into problems, and trying out new ways of behaviour are very much less important than in the studies made by Lewin, Jaques, or Coch and French. Knowledge of fact, as such, matters less here than does the outlook of the group.

For 'freezing' an attitude, therefore, conscious decision and commitment are of great importance and may need to be encouraged (as the popular evangelist knows) even in those groups where discussion has helped in 'unfreezing' a previous attitude; the conscious decision sets the seal on a new way of behaviour.

In the committee

It is amusing and instructive to apply the ideas born in the laboratory to the practical working of a committee. By applying the technical terms with which we have been working to a subject of which everyone has some knowledge, the consistency of the theoretical framework can be tested. The good practitioner, with an untrained but intuitive insight into social process, will recognize that the theory makes sense, in so far as it is any good. Indeed, having read thus far he may have begun to realize that 'the end of all our striving is to arrive where we started, and know the place for the first time'. In so far as the theory is not good, now is the time for its weaknesses to be tested, and this also is a matter for satisfaction. A good wrong theory is one which allows others to put a finger on its faults.

To recapitulate: a good decision is one arrived at after the fullest possible exchange of information and values, and is one to which all members agree. This ensures that all the available facts are taken into consideration and that the morale of the group remains high. A number of functions have to be performed to this end, and techniques are available to achieve it. Responsibility rests on all members of the group, and not on the leader only. Indeed, provided that the necessary functions are carried out, it is a minor matter whether they are carried out by a specially appointed official or not.

The process of steering a proposal through a committee must now be discussed in the light of these considerations. Then attention will be directed more specifically to the normal chairman's functions.

Mr Jones gives notice at some committee meeting, perhaps under 'any other business', that he has been giving some thought to, say, the question of co-opting new members on to the committee and that he hopes to circulate his ideas on the subject to the present members, in the expectation that the matter can be discussed at length on some future occasion. This notifies the others that they will be receiving some communication from him before long, and that his proposal will not be made on a sudden impulse; it will give them time to consider their own ideas on the subject.

After this, he will, if possible, discuss his ideas with the chairman and secretary of his committee, who will be putting the proposal on the agenda for the next meeting. The chairman and secretary are likely to be important and experienced committee members. Good relations in the group demand that they should be consulted early in the proceedings. There may be others in the organization, superior or subordinate, to whom this also applies. It is moreover useful to Mr Jones, for they may be aware of factual aspects of the matter which may not have occurred to him and a discussion will help him to avoid pitfalls he had not envisaged. Co-option to a committee may seem a small matter, but if it changes the balance of power within that committee, a number of people have to be reassured or consulted. It should be said, in passing, that sound ethics and considerations of courtesy require that discussions at this stage be purely at the level of clarification and fact-finding; they are not occasions for canvassing support or for persuasion. Before Jones writes his report he will naturally wish to talk to everyone who can help him to present as co-ordinated and informed a proposal as is possible in the circumstances. It may well be that he has left out some views which others consider important and with which he would not wish to be suddenly confronted at the next committee meeting, where they may easily sway the balance from *pro* to *con*. Difficulties are more easily, and less emotionally, ironed out at this period than at any other. It is even possible that as a result of his informal discussions he will see that his proposal is premature, mistaken, or for some other reason unlikely to gain a majority, in which case he may save his efforts and dignity and withdraw his motion. Nothing harms a current proposal more than the fact that the proposer has had a large number of previous proposals defeated after long arguments. He comes to be regarded as 'not an opinion-leader'.

He therefore sets himself to secure on paper the fullest possible exchange of information and views. His memorandum takes the form of a brief analysis of the present situation, at the end of which he states his proposal. In the next paragraph he lists the advantages and disadvantages of the present position. Then he will show how his proposals will obviate the present disadvantages and procure further advantages. Some difficulties may remain or may even be created by the proposed change. It is wise to state these explicitly, not only so that the fullest information will be provided, but also because it makes it easier in the committee meeting if he is able to show that he understands the objections to his proposal and still feels it worth while to continue. It often seems difficult at a meeting to convince one's opponents that one sees the full force of their objections—to anticipate them on paper saves time later on. It will be noted that after stating his views Mr Jones has to reformulate them in terms of explicit, concrete proposals.

The memorandum is circulated to the committee and other interested parties, as defined in chapter 7. Some other member of the committee may feel sufficiently concerned to circulate his reply, on points where he disagrees. There may indeed be a veritable paperchase. If no reaction is forthcoming, Mr Jones himself may get in touch with some of his fellow-members and ask them for their reactions. The additional information gained in these ways may profoundly affect the proposal that he finally lays before the committee. He has made sure that the committee is as fully informed as lies in his power.

In the committee's discussion of the proposal, much depends on the chairman. A good chairman is the greatest single asset a committee can possess. Unfortunately, not every chairman is ideal. (This is, of course, an additional reason for discussing a proposal with him at length, so that he is at least sure of what is involved. On occasion this may turn almost into a 'briefing meeting', in which Mr Jones makes clear what he wishes to bring out in the discussion and what issues he considers to be less relevant or less pressing.)

Although chairmen may be weak, self-opinionated or stupid, some committees are more handicapped by this than they need be. They tend to use the chairman as a scapegoat for their own lack of skills. It is possible for committee members to take over, in an informal way, some of the chairman's functions, if he is in some respects inadequate. For instance, any member can propose that the motion be now put, and thus attempt to bring the discussion to an end. Or a member may clarify the issue by asking for further information: 'What exactly is it that we are called upon to decide, or have decided, and who is to take action on this decision?' (The secretary will often do this in the normal course of his duties.) Or a member may ask that the discussion be continued at the next meeting because no agreement seems possible at present. This enables the committee to move on to the next item. A committee member may even take over the protective role of the chairman for the sake of good feeling in the group. This is patently not the best way of running a committee, but it is better than letting the whole procedure slide for lack of a *de facto* chairman.

A good chairman ensures that everyone contributes to the discussion. His main function is that of facilitator, though he exercises control by discouraging irrelevancies. Some committee members are notoriously slower than others in grasping points; they will be resentful and unco-operative if they feel, at the time or later, that decisions are being made over their heads or in too great a hurry. It is important, therefore, to see that they are following the arguments and have time to digest and consider what is being said. Sometimes the chairman will speak for a little while without adding materially to the argument, 'padding' in order to allow such members to catch up, or he will allow some other member to do so. The previous circulation of memoranda is also of great help in overcoming this handicap. A chairman should also keep a constant watch for members who have something to contribute but are diffident about breaking into the discussion. He may occasionally call on such members quite explicitly and ask them to give their views. In some ways he will be behaving like the expert faced with a lay-group described earlier in this chapter.

The chairman also keeps order. Speakers often move away from the main point without realizing it and listeners are beguiled into discussing points which do not bear on the decisions to be made. Although some care has necessarily to be taken not to seem overbearing, and some intelligence has to be applied before one can identify with certainty that the point under discussion is in fact irrelevant (and also with due regard to the uses of 'padding'), a moment arrives when it is the chairman's duty to suggest that the point now being discussed might be more usefully brought up again under 'any other business'. To bring the discussion back to the right lines, it is helpful to sum up the (relevant) arguments up to the present moment.

BIBLIOGRAPHY

Allport, G. W., 'Catharsis and the reduction of prejudice', *J. Social Issues* I (1945).

Jaques E., 'Interpretative group discussion as a method of facilitating social change', *Human Relations* I (1947).

Coch L. and French J. R. P., 'Overcoming resistance to change' (1948), in Cartwright and Zander, op. cit., ch. 19.

Lewin K., *Resolving Social Conflicts* (Harper, New York, 1948), and in Cartwright and Zander, op. cit., ch. 21.

Lippitt R., *Training in Community Relations* (Harper, New York, 1949).

Maier N. R. F., 'The quality of group discussion as influenced by a discussion leader', *Human Relations* III (1950).

Cartwright D., 'Achieving change in people', *Human Relations* IV (1951).

Jaques E., *The Changing Culture of a Factory*, op. cit.

Miller N. E., 'Learnable drives and rewards', Stevens S. S. (ed.), *Handbook of Experimental Psychology* (Wiley, New York, 1951), p. 468.

Levine J. and Butler J., 'Lecture *v.* group discussion in changing behaviour' (1952), in Cartwright and Zander, op. cit., ch. 20.

Maier N. R. F. and Solem A. R., 'The contribution of a discussion leader to the quality of group thinking: the effective use of minority opinions' (1952), in Cartwright and Zander, op. cit., ch. 38.

Maier N. R. F., 'An experimental test of the effect of training on discussion leadership', *Human Relations* VI (1953).

Thelen H. A., *Dynamics of Groups at Work* (Chicago U.P., New York, 1954).

Guetzkow H. and Gyr J., 'An analysis of conflict in decision-making groups', *Human Relations* VII (1954).

Bennett E. B., 'Discussion, decision, commitment and consensus in group decision', *Human Relations* VIII (1955).

Ziller R. C., 'Scales of judgment: a determinant of the accuracy of group decision', *Human Relations* VIII (1955).

Seashore S., 'Administrative leadership and organizational effectiveness' and 'The training of leaders for effective human relations', Likert and Hayes, *Some Applications of Behavioural Research* (Unesco Publication, 1956).

Likert R., 'Behavioural research: a guide for effective action', Likert and Hayes, op. cit.

Fox W. M., 'Group reactions to two types of conference leadership', *Human Relations* X (1957).

11

TWO GROUP MEETINGS

*Two verbatim records of group meetings are analysed in terms
of points discussed in previous chapters.*

THE review of the theoretical aspects of working with groups
is now concluded; the rest of this book is concerned with
applying the principles already established. The three final
chapters will do this by training participants in interaction;
the present chapter forms a kind of bridge, using written
records as examples to show what goes on in a group and
how these goings-on may be classified.

Of the two records here presented, one is the invention of a
novelist who is also an industrial psychologist; his intuition in
this field may therefore be trusted to lend verisimilitude. The
other is a shortened version of a tape-recording of a meeting:
it is a verbatim record except that the names and issues have
been changed to preserve anonymity. In each case, the left-
hand side of the page gives the record, and the right-hand side
gives a running commentary in terms of the principles previously outlined. It may be worth while just to review these
principles again.

The first thing to do is to distinguish interaction which is
relevant to the performance of the task from that which is
irrelevant. In a lengthy meeting the distinction between
relevance and irrelevance is not always an easy one to draw,
so it is best to divide the material into a series of 'episodes'.
A new episode begins whenever the problem is redefined
without a protest from any member of the group. In this
way it becomes possible to avoid scoring as irrelevant everything that is said after the first few contributions. For in real
life, people find it hard to stick to the point for long.

The relevant must then be identified in terms of the

categories already established: information, proposal or view, and agreement. The category of 'useful padding' may be added, since more of this is to be expected in real life than in the artificial examples used earlier in the book. Whenever possible, the implied proposals we have called views are to be analysed out into their factual and value components. When the relevance of a contribution is not clear, or when a contribution is clearly irrelevant, this may be attributed to the emotional undercurrents flowing through the group; the contribution should then be analysed in those terms.

At the end of each sequence, the structure of the group is considered in terms explained in chapter 4.

The Board Meeting[1] which follows, has a clearly defined social context; the social pressures are accordingly easy to identify. Spellman is the chairman of the Board of Directors. Lawrence is his son. Walter Lang, whose father founded the business, is the managing director. North is the firm's chief accountant, Talbot-Rees is the sales director, and Martin is in charge of production. Martin is about to retire, his place being taken by Barker, whose first Board Meeting this is. The meeting has been going on for some time.

THE BOARD MEETING

1. *Spellman:* All right. We've elected a new director as per item one, and received the report of the items committee as per item two, and reviewed the production forecast as per item three. The next item is for me to tell my secretary something I've forgotten. And after that we'll take Mr Lang's memorandum.

2. *Lawrence (to Barker):* Have you had a copy of this memorandum of Walter's? (*Walter Lang.*)

[1] Taken from Nigel Balchin, *Sundry Creditors* (Collins, London, 1953), pp. 120 ff.

THE BOARD MEETING

1. *Spellman to group:* Spellman is chairman. He is giving
   information and proposing what should be done. It
   may be argued that since he is telling them what they
   already know this is not strictly task-related. One may
   therefore suggest that the underlying emotional
   function of this contribution is the promotion of good
   feeling and the tiding over from one item of the agenda
   to the next. We may call it 'necessary flannelling'.
   Spellman is very good at this.

Interlude 2–7

between *Lawrence and Barker*. This is task-irrelevant, but
no business is being transacted at this moment.

3. *Barker:* No, Mr Lawrence. I understand they couldn't give me one since it was a Board document.

4. *Lawrence:* But that's bunkum. It concerns you more than anyone else, or soon will.

5. *Barker:* I've seen Mr Martin's.

6. *Lawrence:* Ah—I see. The correct procedure. What do you think of it?

7. *Barker:* Well . . . I've got some figures that I've given to Mr Martin.

8. *Spellman:* Right. Errors and omissions dealt with. Item four—the managing director's memorandum. You've all seen this. It's a memorandum on the broad future of the business. Mr Lang's view is (correct me if I've got anything wrong, Walter)—Mr Lang feels that the future of the business lies, or should lie, in more concentration on our own products, and less fabricating for other people. I venture to suggest that nobody is going to disagree with that.

9. *Talbot-Rees:* Hear, hear.

10. *Spellman:* In fact, I never can remember anybody disagreeing with it, and it's been coming up every so often for the last thirty years. We all know that the outside fabricating jobs are a nuisance. Nobody in their senses would want them if he could get something else. But the principle has always been that we'd get rid of them when we could see how to make our normal turnover and profit without them. What's new in Mr Lang's memorandum, as I understand it, is that he wants to get rid of them anyhow, whether we can see immediately what to put in their place or not. That so, Walter?

11. *Lang:* More or less.

12. *Spellman:* All right. Well now, gentlemen, I asked Mr Lang to speak to his memorandum and explain what he's got in mind.

Emotional function: friendly self-expression on Lawrence's part. Barker confines himself to neutral statements of information and does not respond to Lawrence's invitations to express his feelings. Expressions like 'bunkum' and 'ah . . . the correct procedure' reveal Lawrence's somewhat frivolous contempt for the actions of other members of the group.

Back to business 8–27

8. *Spellman to group.* Relevant. Gives information. General impression of good and genial chairman. *To Lang* asks relevant information.

9. *Talbot-Rees to Spellman:* Irrelevant to task performance. Emotional function: expression of friendliness.

10. *Spellman to group.* Still a typical chairman's speech, see comments above.
   To Lang: asks information (a sensible way of introducing Lang—encouraging him to put his point of view).

11. *Lang to Spellman:* Relevant. Gives information but a bare minimum.

12. *Spellman to Lang:* Relevant. Makes proposal.

13. *Lang:* I don't want to talk very much. It's all set out here. The chairman has told you we've wanted to get rid of fabricating contracts for thirty-five years. I'm suggesting that we should get rid of them in the next two—that by the end of 1955 we should be working solely on our own patented products. I've tried to show how that might be done without much loss of profit. But the main thing is the principle that we put this through whether we lose turnover and profit or not. As long as we go messing on with the fabricating work, there's no real incentive for anybody to get on and develop our stuff. If our bread and butter depend on it, it'll be different.

14. *Spellman:* You reckon the best way to teach us to swim is to pitch us into ten foot of water, eh?

15. *Lang:* That's right, Mr Chairman.

16. *Spellman:* Well then, gentlemen, the discussion is open. I've got my own views about this, but I'd rather hear someone else first.

pause

17. *North:* I don't want this to be taken as . . . as an observation on Mr Lang's memorandum, Mr Chairman, and still less as a criticism. But I've taken out a few figures which might help in the discussion. . . . The average rate of net profit on fabricating work was only 5 per cent. On our own products side, it was just over 14 per cent.

18. *Lang:* And mind you, that's when the patent side is still about a quarter efficient.

13. *Lang to group:* Relevant; gives information, expresses views and makes proposal. Now that a proposal has been made, all contributions must be assessed not only as relevant or irrelevant to the task, but also as favourable or unfavourable as regards the proposal. Clearly when Lang speaks it will be in favour of his own proposal.

14. *Spellman to Lang:* Request for view or hostile self-expression? Lang can choose which way he will take it. The emotional tone sounds genial but is adverse to Lang's proposal.

15. *Lang to Spellman:* Lang chooses to regard it as strictly relevant. This is one way of dealing with questions of this kind. Gives information.

16. *Spellman to group:* Relevant. Asks for views: a chairman's function.

withdrawal by group

17. *North to group* (addressing chair is conventional): 'I don't want . . .' is irrelevant; its emotional significance is partly propitiatory, largely withdrawal from committing himself. Gives relevant information in favour of Lang's proposal. North is performing his function as expert (chief accountant).

18. *Lang to group:* Relevant view.

19. *North:* I agree, sir. (*Turns over a page.*) But on the other side, of the *total* net profit, 58 per cent came from the fabricating work and only 42 per cent from our own products. I thought the Board might like to have these figures in front of them. The relative turnover figures are about 80 per cent fabricating and 20 per cent own product.

20. *Spellman* (*to Lang*)*:* You accept these figures?

21. *Lang:* Of course. They *are* my case. Twenty per cent of your turnover gives you nearly half your profit.

22. *Lawrence:* Hey—wait a minute . . . ⎫
23. *Martin:* But . . .   ⎬ *together.*
                                                          ⎭

24. *Spellman:* George? (*George Martin.*)

25. *Martin:* I was only going to say that perhaps that's rather too simple a way of looking at it. After all, the fabricating may only show 5 per cent net, but that's after it's paid 80 per cent of your overheads.

26. *Lawrence:* In fact, without the fabricating work, we should run at a loss.

27. *North:* Oh, naturally.

28. *Lang:* This is just what we've been doing for thirty years and what I'm asking you to stop. Nobody needs trot out these figures as though they were a discovery, or to remind me there are such things as overheads.

29. *Spellman:* Yes?

30. *Lang:* Well then, can we stop talking about what the business used to be or is now, and start talking of what it's *going* to be?

19. *North to Lang:* Agrees. *To group:* further relevant information, this time against Lang's proposal. North does not align himself with either side. He does not combine facts and values. He is an expert in his own field, not a co-ordinator.

20. *Spellman to Lang:* Asks for relevant information. A chairman's function.

21. *Lang to group:* Gives information and view. He interprets North's figures as favourable to his case.

22.⎫ *Lawrence and Martin* imply disagreement with Lang's
23.⎭ view.

24. *Spellman to Martin:* Relevant, asks for views.

25. *Martin to group:* 'I was only . . .' irrelevant, function as for North in 17. The rest is relevant: a view against Lang's case.

26. *Lawrence to group:* Relevant information, but no more than a restatement of Martin's contribution. Emotional function: to make it quite clear that the information runs against Lang.

27. *North to group:* Relevant information.

Interlude on values 28–41

28.⎫ *Lang to group:* If this is information, its relevance to the
30.⎭ problem in hand is not at once clear. The first sentence may be interpreted as a statement of values, and by implication a proposal that these values should govern the decision. The second sentence is certainly irrelevant and an expression of hostility. The third sentence (30) is a proposal as to governing principles.

31. *Lawrence:* Forgive me, Mr Chairman, but I'm getting a
    bit lost. I understood that the managing director's
    whole point was that he wanted to scrap the fabricating
    work more or less as . . . as a matter of *principle*, so to
    speak?

32. *Spellman:* Well, I rather understood that myself. But, of
    course . . .

33. *Lawrence:* Then surely Mr North's figures are extremely
    relevant. Perhaps they're the reason *why* we've wanted
    to do this for thirty years and haven't done it? To talk
    about scrapping the work that gives us 80 per cent of
    our turnover. . . .

34. *Talbot-Rees:* Oh come, surely we can assume that the
    managing director didn't mean it like *that*. . . .

35. *Lang:* I've got the use of my senses even if some of you
    seem to doubt it.

36. *Talbot-Rees:* Quite. As I read it, this memorandum merely
    suggests that in order to carry out the change-over, we
    should be prepared, if necessary, to accept some
    sacrifices. Do I interpret you rightly?

37. *Lang:* Of course.

38. *Spellman:* Right. Then the obvious question is, what are
    the sacrifices likely to amount to? Nobody's likely to
    object if we reckon net profit's likely to fall by 10 per
    cent for a few years. And nobody's likely to agree if
    it's going to fall by 50 per cent.

39. *Lang:* Why not?

40. *Spellman:* Very well. Mr Lang would consider even
    50 per cent.

41. *Lang:* In fact, according to my calculations, there'd be
    very little loss of profit after the first two years, and
    by the fifth year profit would be back to normal. And
    what's more, you'd have a worth-while business instead
    of a lot of odds and ends.

31. *Lawrence to group:* Relevant request for information, which explores Lang's view that a decision should be reached mainly on grounds of principle. The undertone is hostile to Lang.

32. *Spellman to Lawrence:* Relevance not strictly clear, but certainly there is friendly support for Lawrence.

33. *Lawrence to group:* Relevant view: profit not principle should govern the decision.

34. *Talbot-Rees to group:* Relevant view (relevant in that it affects the group's understanding of Lang's proposal).

35. *Lang to group:* Irrelevant expression of hostility.

36. *Talbot-Rees to Lang:* Gives relevant information (restatement of proposal in more moderate terms). Asks for information.

37. *Lang to Talbot-Rees:* Gives the information asked for.

38. *Spellman to group:* Asks for views: a proper chairman's function. The value in question is profitability in a few years' time.

39. *Lang to Spellman:* Disagrees with the value-element in Spellman's contribution. Profitability in a few years' time is not his governing value.

40. *Spellman to group:* Relevant: corrects previous information. Note that he keeps the discussion cool by confining himself to facts: no self-expression here.

41. *Lang to group:* Relevant: information and view. He reiterates the main value governing his proposal.

42. *Spellman:* Then what we want to know now is, how far the Board accepts Mr Lang's calculations as approximately correct or likely to be fulfilled, or possible to fulfil. First of all, can we produce the stuff? George, is this you? (*George Martin.*)

43. *Martin:* Well, Mr Chairman, I shall be gone, so . . .

laughter

. . . but Barker and I have been through this and we think there are several things the Board ought to realize from the production side. First of all, out of the six patent jobs Mr Lang mentions, only two are in production, and three are only experimental. Take a thing like the paint-spray gun. We think we're on to something. But we may not be. I certainly wouldn't like to guarantee we could depend on that as a big line.

44. *Lang:* Don't forget that I'm asking that you have a proper experimental department, George. Not two men and a cat.

45. *Martin:* Even so, sir, we don't *know* it's any good. Then take plant. There's bound to be a heavy capital expenditure tooling up, of course. But how about getting machine tools? There's plant now that we've had on order for three years. And it's not getting any better. Then we all know about steel. . . .

46. *Lang:* I thought we should come to steel soon.

47. *Martin:* Taking it all in all, there's a lot of real headaches here. I don't say we couldn't do it eventually. But I'm afraid it'd take a lot longer than's suggested here. (*To Barker*): You check?

Back to business 42–52

42. *Spellman to group:* At this point the discussion reverts to the main proposal. No agreement has been reached, however, on the subsidiary problem of the values involved. This will make difficulties later on. Relevant request for information. *To Martin:* Relevant request for information or views.

43. *Martin to group:* Irrelevant, its emotional function is friendly.

tension-relief

Gives relevant information, on the whole against Lang's proposal.

44. *Lang to Martin:* It is not clear whether this is relevant or not. In any case, the emotional significance is to counter Martin's pessimism. His main value is restated in more popular terms.

45. *Martin to Lang:* Gives relevant view, against Lang's proposal. Martin has chosen to treat Lang's contribution as information. Martin is the only expert who commits himself. He can more easily afford to do so since he will be retiring.

46. *Lang to group:* Irrelevant. Expresses hostility. (Steel is not irrelevant, but what he says about it is.)

47. *Martin to group:* Relevant view, against proposal. *To Barker:* Relevant request for information or view.

48. *Barker:* Yes, sir. I don't think a plan like this could be carried through under present conditions in less than ten years.

49. *Lang:* Oh bunkum.

50. *Spellman:* Well, that's the opinion of the production side. How about selling the stuff if we could make it? Talbot-Rees?

51. *Talbot-Rees:* Well, sir—I should like to pay a tribute to the ... the quality of *vision* that has gone into this memorandum. As a salesman, it thrills and challenges me. And I can only say that if the plan is adopted, the sales side will throw themselves into it heart and soul.

52. *Spellman:* Quite. But could you sell the stuff?

53. *Talbot-Rees:* With respect, Mr Chairman, that's hardly a possible question.

54. *Lawrence:* How long is a piece of string? You're asking him if he can sell something that doesn't exist, at a price not stated, at some unknown date in the future.

55. *Lang:* Well, we're asking *him*.

56. *Lawrence:* Sorry, Mr Chairman.

57. *Talbot-Rees:* I see nothing *impossible* in Mr Lang's figures. But naturally it depends on so many factors.

58. *Lang:* I asked you about every one of those figures before I put them down.

59. *Talbot-Rees:* You did, sir. And I answered that they were not impossible given that the article was right, the price was right and the state of the market favourable. I stand by that.

60. *Lang:* Why is it that neither production nor sales people have ever got the courage of their convictions?

61. *Lawrence:* It's just that they haven't got the courage of *your* convictions.

long pause

48. *Barker to Martin:* Relevant view and agreement. The competing values of short-term and long-term profitability are here explicit.

49. *Lang to Barker:* Relevant. Agrees in a disagreeable way.

50. *Spellman to group:* Relevant information. (Summing-up is a chairman's function.) *To Talbot-Rees:* Asks for view.

51. *Talbot-Rees to Lang:* Irrelevant expression of friendliness. (His feelings are irrelevant to the proposal under discussion.)

52. *Spellman to Talbot-Rees:* Asks for relevant information. (Note 'but' which is expressive in this context, however.)

Interlude: the expert and decision-making 53–61

Talbot-Rees can sell goods. He is an expert in this. Business decisions must be made in conditions of uncertainty. To do this requires another kind of skill. The expert is not always skilled in this kind of decision-making as well. Talbot-Rees is incapable of making such decisions. Lawrence understands this. He is by temperament not a decision-maker. Spellman and Lang, who are, do not understand this. Thus Spellman tries to make Talbot-Rees commit himself against the proposal, and Lang for it. They are organizational experts: co-ordinators. The hostility between Lang and Lawrence is clearly revealed in this passage.

60. *Lang to group:* Irrelevant, expresses hostility to those who have let him down.

61. *Lawrence to Lang:* Irrelevant. Expresses hostility. (See 55.)

withdrawal

62. *Spellman:* Well, gentlemen—the sense of the meeting seems to be this. We all accept the principle behind the managing director's memorandum. And we admire the vision and force with which he has expressed his ideas—as he always does. But on the production and sales side, there are a lot of question marks. This is too big a thing to go rushing into in the dark. We may not be altogether satisfied with the business, but it's sound and it's profitable. As directors, we certainly should not be justified in giving up the substance for the shadow. But that doesn't mean we want to sit still and do nothing. We must get on with this change-over as fast as is prudent. So I suggest that we, as a Board, say to the managing director that we support and offer every encouragement to the principle he has expressed; and that we are prepared to taper off the fabricating work just as quickly as the development of the patents producing side is able to replace the loss of turnover and profit, or the greater part of it. How about that?

63. *Lang:* With all respect, Mr Chairman, that's no use to me at all.

64. *Spellman (rather blankly):* Oh.

65. *Lang:* It leaves us exactly where we were.

66. *Spellman:* But I said . . .

67. *Lang:* It's no use saying things. We've got to *do* things. And this is just a formula for doing nothing.

68. *Spellman:* I don't agree for a moment.

69. *Lawrence:* Are you still asking the Board to accept this memorandum exactly as it stands, Walter? Because . . .

Back to business 62–70

62. *Spellman to group:* Gives views, expresses friendliness to Lang, makes proposal. (See also comments on items 1, 8, and 10.) His proposal is an attempt to reconcile the facts and conflicting values into an acceptable whole. But the competing claims of long-term and short-term profitability are glossed over. The conflict over values has not been brought to an explicit conclusion.

63. *Lang to group:* Gives relevant view.

65. *Lang to Spellman:* Gives relevant information (amplifies 63).

67. *Lang to group:* A further amplification, therefore relevant, view. But not an effective contribution. Perhaps a proposal is implied to carry out his plans after all?

68. *Spellman to Lang:* Disagrees.

69. *Lawrence to Lang:* Asks for relevant information. (Note use of first name here.)

70. *Lang:* Gentlemen, my father founded this business. I think I'm right in saying that today I'm the largest individual shareholder in it. I've run the business for the last fifteen years and what I've done with it is there on the accounts for everybody to see. When I put up a considered memorandum, like this, I don't expect it to be dismissed after a quarter of an hour's amateur discussion. There are some of us here who . . .

71. *Spellman (quietly):* I don't think we shall get anywhere like this, Walter.

72. *Lang (furiously):* I refuse to be impeded at every step by . . .

73. *Spellman:* Nobody's trying to impede you.

74. *Lang:* No, and they'd better not try. (*Walks out.*)

75. *Spellman:* Well—I think we'd better adjourn.

76. *Lawrence (to Barker):* You mustn't be disappointed if it isn't always as amusing as this.

From the interaction-matrix on p. 152 it will be seen that Spellman, as chairman, elicits information and views markedly more frequently than the others. He gives information almost as often as Lang—this is to be expected from a man of his experience and grasp. Two of his proposals are on procedure; the third is a counter-proposal to Lang's.

Lang is bound to speak a lot, because he is the one who wants to introduce an innovation. He engages twice in hostile self-expression, and twice he disagrees openly with other members of the group.

The technical experts in this firm are of somewhat lower status. This shows itself, for instance, in the fact that they address Spellman and Lang as 'sir', while they themselves are addressed genially by their first names. (The anarchic Lawrence, of course, speaks to all in the same manner.) Spellman, Lawrence, and Lang are on the Board by virtue of their family position; the others are there because of their technical expertise—as such they have a right to be heard, but little personal power.

This lack of standing shows itself also in the curious little

Final interlude: the explosion

70. *Lang to group:* Note that he interrupts. His contribution is
    irrelevant, but it is a moving expression of disappoint-
    ment and hostility.
    The emotional significance of this explosion is quite
    clear.

75. *Spellman to group:* Proposes to end meeting.
76. *Lawrence to Barker:* One final frivolous remark: friendly
    to Barker, withdrawal from group.

---

propitiatory gambit in which North and Martin engage before
they make their main point: it is a sort of withdrawal from
responsibility.

North confines himself to information: he utters no views.
Martin is able to contribute in a greater variety of ways. He
commits himself to a view on Lang's proposal, and at one
point implies disagreement with Lang. Spellman encourages
Lang, being aware of his alignment. Martin's willingness to
stand his ground may be connected with his long experience
in the firm, and with his imminent retirement.

The author has made Talbot-Rees almost too emphatically
a salesman, cheerful, smooth, anxious to keep human relations
cordial. He is remarkable for expressing warmth to both of
the opposing parties.

The I-we-you table is less enlightening here than it can
sometimes be, though it is interesting to note that the use of
the first person singular is markedly more frequent here than
it is, for instance, in the more relaxed atmosphere of the grant-
episode in chapter 4. Lang's frequent use of 'you', as though
the group is external to himself, is also worthy of note.

Interaction-matrix

	Spellman	Lawrence	Lang	Talbot-Rees	North	Martin	Barker	Group
Spellman		agr+	inf+ 3 inf− vi+ 3 vi− agr− exp+f	2 vi−		2 vi−		5 inf+ inf−, vi+ 2 vi− 3 pro+ exp+f
Lawrence			inf− agr− (imp)					inf− vi+
Lang	agr−						agr−	7 inf+ inf− 7 vi+ 2 pro+ 2 exp−h
Talbot-Rees			inf− exp+f					2 inf+ vi+ exp+f
North			agr+					3 inf+ exp−w
Martin			agr− (imp)				vi−	inf+, vi+ exp+f exp−w
Barker						agr+		vi+

I-we-you table

		Total number of contributions	I	we	you
Spellman ..	..	21	15	22	5
Lawrence	..	8	3	4	1
Lang	..	23	10	14	9
Talbot-Rees	..	7	4	2	1
North	..	3	4	2	0
Martin	..	5	6	8	2
Barker	..	1	1	0	0

The figures for the interaction-matrix and the I-we-you table are to some extent a matter of interpretation and must therefore be taken as indicative rather than rigorously accurate. Episodes 2–7 are excluded.

The Committee Meeting which now follows may be assumed to be the first meeting of a number of local tradesmen who feel that they are being harassed by too much advice and interference from London, not only by government departments, but also by bodies with no official standing, in particular by the British Council for the Promotion of Hygienic Foodstuffs—the Hygiene Council for short. A chairman has been elected, and Mr Strang, a local man with close connections with the Hygiene Council, on the Board of which he sits, has been invited to attend.

1. *Chairman:* We are meeting today to discuss ways and means by which we can put this committee on the map. London has had its own way far too long. It is time that Bristol showed that it has plenty of initiative and does not need these directives and pieces of advice that London seems to think we need in order to keep us up to scratch.

2. *Ely:* Before we discuss that point, Mr Chairman, I would like to say that my own organization is fully in agreement with the spirit in which this committee was set up and they would like to support it. There is, however, one small point that I want to draw attention to. On page 3 of the minutes, line 22, it is written that 'centralization is at the root of our difficulties and the first problem that must be dealt with'. Now although it is true that in the field of control over our products the people in London have interfered far too much, on the whole we can benefit a good deal from a centralized authority. Indeed my own organization is centred on London and we have never had difficulties of that kind with them. I had a sticky moment at the last Board meeting to explain what must have been in the mind of the secretary when that sentence was written.

3. *Hands:* On the subject of minutes, Mr Chairman, do we want to have them sent out in their present form to all organizations whether they have members on this committee or not? It seems to me we run a great risk of leakage if we allow all our discussions to be so generally known. I suggest that it would be better if minutes were not circulated beforehand, but read from the book at the beginning of the meeting.

4. *Pope:* With reference to that point, I should like to say that these committee meetings go on long enough without prolonging them unnecessarily by reading the minutes in a form acceptable to all.

1. *Chairman to group:* Gives relevant information and views. The value being implied is very clear: Bristol should show that it is independent of London.

The search for a topic

2. *Ely to group:* (Chairman conventionally addressed.) Irrelevant to the task, however vaguely stated. This should go under A.O.B. as the chairman quite properly suggests under 5. What can the emotional significance be? Pure self-expression. This seems unnecessary flannelling.

3. *Hands to group:* This is irrelevant both to Ely and to chairman's statement of the task. Emotional significance: self-expression on Hands' part, presumably annoyance on Ely's whose question remains unanswered.

4. *Pope to Hands:* View relevant to Hands, although not to task as stated by chairman. Some hostility to the whole meeting implied?

5. *Chairman:* This is an interesting and rather tricky problem. Perhaps we should leave it for the time being, and, if we can, consider it later this afternoon under A.O.B. We are examining item four on the agenda, plans for the future of the new committee.

6. *Truck:* There are probably two conflicting principles in-volved—and this is most important in my submission. One is that people who can get together fairly easily should meet. The Grocers have their own pretty closely knit organization and I believe they have a representative on the London council. This group was formed in 1949–50 and I have been closely connected with their work. I think we can leave them to look after them-selves. In the case of the Cardiff people again they have their own organization and I think we should tie up with them.

7. *Ely:* I hope we will not spend too much time on matters of formality but rather use the time to endeavour to see what can be done in the group now and so put the flag up by doing something actively and building round that nucleus. Questions of name and membership will be solved if we can only agree on some action. This group is gathering in strength as it goes on, already ten organizations are represented on this committee and that is enough to make a start.

8. *Brewer:* There are two industries which I feel we should seriously consider. One: chemists, and two: laundries. Perhaps Mr Strang would be prepared to act in the interests of the latter?

9. *Strang:* I don't think I could possibly put myself forward as a representative of the laundry trades. I don't know to what extent they are grouped together or if they have any kind of organization. I come here to represent myself and the London body and nothing else at all. I do feel, though, that greengrocers and fishmongers ought to be represented when matters of hygiene are

5. *Chairman to group:* Makes relevant proposal. Note the mildness of his approach throughout. He stops the Hands-Pope dispute becoming serious, and recalls the meeting to the main purpose.

The question of membership

6. *Truck to group:* Relevance not clear. Meaning not clear: what are the two conflicting principles? Function—self-expression; unnecessary flannelling. Nevertheless, a new problem is stated and the other members take it up: who should attend their meetings? This whole discussion looks to the outsider irrelevant, since it does not further the main problem as stated by the chairman, but scored as view and proposal.

7. *Ely to group:* Relevant to the new discussion on membership. Also a general note of encouragement and good feeling conveyed. But note also that he has headed off Truck and any clarification or discussion of his point. General point of view: to do something (undefined) quickly and not to worry about membership.

8. *Brewer to group and Strang:* Relevant proposals. Makes two suggestions. Value: membership is an important question.

9. *Strang to group and Brewer:* Relevant. Disagrees with previous view, giving information in explanation. Makes another kind of proposal. This proposal is the first really relevant contribution to the task as defined by chairman in 1. Values: democratic and hygienic.

being discussed. Complaints, of which many I am sure are unjustified, have been seen in the Press about their standards of cleanliness and they ought to have a chance to discuss the matter.

10. *Hands:* I suggest that we get our organizations to pay for the salaries of three inspectors to whose inspection we can all submit ourselves. Then they can fight it out with the London people and in any argument our hands will be much strengthened.

11. *Blank:* I wholeheartedly support Mr Hands' proposal. We've been on friendly terms for a long time now and our organizations have always co-operated most cordially. I know my own organization will do what it can to support the work of this new committee, but, frankly, I am afraid that they will not be very pleased to be asked to fork out money at this stage in the proceedings. I think we ought first of all show what we can do and that we deserve the money. Money is tight and there are a great number of causes to which it may go.

12. *Pope:* Hear, hear. I don't think we ought to be doing anything that would commit our organizations to financial contribution. We must be very careful not to be too ambitious and then go flop. A small slow start is the surest way to success. Let me see—dear me, the contributions would have to be heavy, very heavy indeed, to pay for such a scheme.

13. *Truck:* I think we should explore the possibilities that have been opened before us and I must say I think Mr Hands' proposal a very good one. On the other hand, as Mr Pope so wisely said, we must contrive to keep the support of the trade associations, and although they send representatives now, they would not really like us to go back and say we want money for something that may or may not be successful.

14. *Hands:* Could we perhaps . . . I think . . .

A proposal concerning finance

10. *Hands to group:* Makes proposal relevant to the main issue but not to the question of membership now under discussion. It is taken up by the others only in its financial aspect. Value: high standards must be demonstrably upheld. Outside reference-group: London.

11. *Blank to Hands:* Relevant in the agreement/disagreement category. His first sentence shows agreement with Hands, his second positive expression towards him, but the sense of his contribution is that he disagrees with Hands' proposal. Friendliness to Hands is scored, as well as views. Values: economy and caution. Outside reference-group: his own firm

12. *Pope to group and Blank:* Relevant. Agrees with Blank, thus disagreeing with Hands. His values are those of Blank's: economy and caution. Outside reference-group: his own firm.

13. *Truck to Hands and Pope:* Irrelevant. Agrees, but with both previous speakers and so does not contribute in any way to progress of task. But his values are theirs: economy and caution. Outside reference-group: theirs. Scored as friendliness as well as views.

15. *Kelly:* Part of our difficulty, I think, is the fact that this is really a self-appointed body. We are not representative and we are still much too small to stand up to London. Perhaps we ought to draw up our aims and a programme and send it round to all trade associations. That way we can recruit members and the financial burden will be less.

16. *Carter:* Speaking as a representative of the Bristol and Somerset Confectioners' Association, I have only just been informed that this committee has come into existence. I fully support and approve of the existence of this committee. I don't think that we should engage in any activity which we cannot work together at, either as members or as an association. Although I do not think my association would wish to associate itself with the proposal, I am sure it will support this group very actively in any way it can.

17. *Truck:* May I ask, Mr Chairman, if there is a proposal before the committee at the moment?

18. *Chairman:* There is none, but I should welcome one.

19. *Brewer:* I think we ought to thank the chairman for allowing the meetings to take place in his office. It is not very easy to find a place which all members can attend with equal ease, but certainly this is very convenient for us. And indeed, we ought to thank the chairman for all his good work in connection with this group.

20. *Ely:* It seems to me that we have had a lot of expressions of opinion and a lot of ideas. But we are talking, all of us, rather loosely and we really have got to decide and make up our mind what the object of the whole thing is. Whether we are here to endeavour to put the Council of Hygiene on lines which we think are not only socially admirable —which undoubtedly they already are—but also commercially satisfactory to the manufacturers and retailers.

A new proposal incorporating both previous topics (membership and finance)

15. *Kelly to group:* Relevant to question of membership and finance, but not to the main purpose. Interrupts Hands, who might have had something definite to say. Kelly is secretary and thus cautious speaker. He gives information on the nature of the task and bases a procedural proposal on this information; scored as view.

16. *Carter to group:* Irrelevant, since it adds nothing to the task. Moreover, it sidetracks the meeting just when it might have pulled itself together. Emotional function for Carter: self-expression. Outside reference-group: the Bristol and Somersetshire Confectionery Association. Main value probably also the B. & S.C.A. Not scored.

17. *Truck to Chairman:* Relevant request for information. Attempts to pull meeting together.

18. *Chairman to group:* Relevant information (though not quite correct). Requests proposals, scored as request for views.

19. *Brewer to Chairman:* Irrelevant friendliness. Underlying this contribution may be Brewer's feeling that the Chair has been slighted by Truck 'bullying the chairman'.

20. *Ely to group:* More or less relevant views. Proposes that the main purpose be discussed. Value: to do something (undefined). Outside reference-groups: manufacturers and retailers.

21. *Truck:* I agree.

22. *Blank:* I think we must get down to what the objects are, and when we are a bit clearer about that then we perhaps can . . .

23. *Strang:* Of course one thing which we must keep in mind is that in London the President of the Hygiene Council has been able to persuade the Treasury to lend them facilities for a research centre where a good job of educating not only the public but also the manufacturers and retailers can be done. I think it is better not to divide our forces but to use that centre to which people from the West could come. There would be no point in duplicating their work.

24. *Hands:* I think we should write to the London Council. After all, this is public money—the ratepayers' money—and to spend half a million or so on what a clique in London with fancy ideas . . .

25. *Strang:* I don't know that I would put it as strongly as that. These are very highly qualified people who . . .

26. *Hands:* But I do put it like that, Strang. I think you should make the strongest possible recommendation . . .

27. *Ely:* Hear, hear.

28. *Pope:* Mr. Chairman, I should like to know, as a matter of public interest, how far this matter has gone.

29. *Strang:* If I may answer that question, Mr Chairman. Some six months ago we—I mean the London Council —first approached . . .

30. *Pope:* Then I should like to ask Mr Strang, through you, Mr Chairman, how it is that we have only just had this matter come to our ears.

31. *Strang:* I am not saying I know, but if I did I don't think I am at liberty to tell you.

32. *Ely:* These aren't private perquisites, these things should be publicized.

21. *Truck to Ely:* Relevant. Agrees.
22. *Blank to group:* Relevant but not really helpful view.

The scapegoat

23. *Strang to group:* Gives relevant information and makes a proposal. All members except Blank now one by one turn on Strang, supporting each other. The precise interaction pattern of this emotional interlude is not of present interest. Hands, who starts the attack, has already had three suggestions turned down. Whenever Strang speaks he makes matters worse. The emotional significance of this interlude is that for the first time the members feel really involved. They blow off steam after the frustration of finding no solution to their problem. Note that Strang represents the very body they oppose, and that now they have something definite to discuss there is really a remarkable amount of information exchange.

Note the significant 'we' and its correction.

33. *Truck:* Most decidedly so. Imagine a meeting of the District Council doing things in the General Purposes Committee and keeping the public from knowing. It is a matter that concerns us all. It isn't the perquisite of any members, or the members as a whole, of the Council of Hygiene. These things belong to us.

34. *Strang:* As a member of the London Council, Mr Truck, I am not empowered to go round and tell you what I was told by the . . .

35. *Brewer:* These things should be as a matter of courtesy publicized by the Council themselves. I am sorry to see Mr Strang so unshakable on this issue.

36. *Chairman:* I think perhaps we ought to be discussing a definite proposal and come to some conclusion.

37. *Ely:* The best thing we can do as I see it is to attempt to raise our own standard of hygiene. Then we can argue with London from our own strengths and not from weakness. The proposal made by Mr Hands, earlier on, is ideal, but I think we shall not reach that stage for a little while. But I have heard of a very successful set of meetings which the Scottish Retailers put on—of course they have their own problems—quiz meetings at which packaging and wrapping in a particular line of goods was discussed and the advantages and disadvantages considered. Many alterations were made as a result. It was most successful and the standards were raised a good deal.

38. *Hands:* I think that is a very good suggestion and I support it wholeheartedly. My own association, which has perhaps very special facilities in this line, would, I am sure, welcome such a meeting on its premises and would probably extend catering facilities as well.

Omnes: Hear, hear, very good, that's fine, etc.

Final episode—proposal and decision

36. *Chairman to group:* View relevant to main task. He cuts the quarrel off and recalls the meeting to order.

37. *Ely to group:* Relevant to main task. Gives information and views. Following chairman's lead. Is he continuing contribution 20? His proposal seems to embody all the values implied in the main discussion: economy, democracy, hygiene, caution. Outside reference-groups: London's Hygiene Council; the Scottish Retailers' Association.

38. *Hands to group and Ely:* Relevant. Agrees with Ely, gives information and further proposal.

39. *Truck:* It seems that we are getting somewhere. We are all very grateful, I am sure, to Mr Ely and Mr Hands for their suggestions. I think perhaps the first one could take place in September.

40. *Chairman:* Will someone put a formal proposition?

Final details are then settled quickly and efficiently.

41. *Carter:* I personally feel very strongly, and I think it is other people's opinion as well, that while we are striking out to help some little independence it is far more our wish that we can be in harmony and in tune with the Council of Hygiene. If they will permit us and if we are sensible enough to see our way to do this, it will be to our mutual advantage. In any sense, suggesting at any particular stage that our first wish is to be up against the Council, or to act entirely on our own, is a mistake.

42. *Blank:* I am sure that is the general opinion and I hope that Mr Strang personally does really feel that. That is really the essence of the matter. It is a matter of how you approach the problem.

43. *Hands:* I don't think we ought to allow ourselves to be labelled as running in any way antagonistic to the Council of Hygiene. We are not, definitely not. What we are doing is to try and initiate something that we feel ought to be done. The fact that the Council of Hygiene is not doing it is by the way. If they can help us or we can help them at any time, so much the better, but here is something that we here—as manufacturers and retailers—feel should be done and we are setting about doing it, and I do think it could be fatal to set up any idea that this is a counter-move to the Council of Hygiene, because it is not.

44. *Strang:* Thank you very much, Mr Hands, that puts it very, very clearly and the way I like to think of it.

39. *Truck to group, Ely, and Hands:* Relevant proposal. He is giving general support. Irrelevant positive expression of sentiment, to Ely and Hands.

40. *Chairman to group:* Relevant, asks for proposal.

Relations with Strang and with London

41. *Carter to group:* Views relevant to the problem of the scapegoat-episode. Encourages good feeling all round. Value: harmony with outside group. There follows now another interlude of mainly emotional significance, pouring balm on the wounds which they inflicted on Strang. Having come to a satisfactory conclusion, they can afford to do this; Strang himself is less aggressive than before.

42. *Blank to Strang:* Agrees with Carter. Friendliness to Strang.

43. *Hands to group:* Repeats Carter's view that the group should not set up in overt opposition to the Hygiene Council.

44. *Strang to Hands:* Agrees and expresses warmth.

45. *Pope:* Mr Chairman, under any other business, would it be right and proper, rather than put the onus on Mr Strang here, to write a letter to the Council of Hygiene asking them if they can give us information as to how far they have gone with their new plans?

46. *Chairman:* That is agreed.

47. *Ely:* No, it is not.

48. *Brewer:* I thought, Mr Chairman, that it was agreed that we should accept the suggestion previously agreed upon that we write to the Treasury about this matter, and that as far as the Council is concerned, we seek to act through our representative Mr Strang, seeking to get a two-way traffic in ideas started that way.

49. *Strang:* Mr Chairman, I don't think we . . .

50. *Brewer:* If I could just finish that off by saying that I now take a rather different view of what Mr Strang has to tell us. I rather feel, with all due respect to Mr Pope and Mr Hands, that Mr Strang is not in a position to tell us. But the Council as a whole should be able to tell us.

51. *Strang:* I was only going to say, merely my own hunch, but I feel that it would be a mistake to write to the Treasury. Such a letter would come back to the Council, who might consider it a rather standoffish and a rather unfriendly act. Any letter to the Council itself, splendid. I mean I think it would carry a great deal more weight than merely my saying it, but if you write to the Treasury, well, you have got civil servants in charge there and it rather looks as though you are trying to wave a spear in their faces. I don't think that would have the effect you want.

52. *Pope:* I think Mr Strang is right and we should follow his advice. How would it be to take the first move by writing to the Council of Hygiene? Mr Strang will follow that up next week at the London Council meeting and see what happens. We don't want to start

45. *Pope to group:* Relevant, asks for views. Value: further information (before exercising pressure).

46. *Chair to group:* Gives relevant information.

47. *Ely to Chair:* Relevant. Gives further information.

48. *Brewer to group:* Gives relevant information.

50. *Brewer to group:* If relevant, gives information about his feelings only. Gives relevant view. Values: Strang must be protected from his indiscretions but further information must be obtained.

51. *Strang to group:* Gives relevant information and makes proposal (deferentially). Value: the preservation of harmony in all relations.

52. *Pope to group:* Gives relevant view and makes proposal backing Strang, with whom he agrees.

inserting the corkscrew. Let's start by trying the ordinary friendly methods and see what happens.

53. *Chairman:* I suggest Mr Strang knows our opinion and I think we should show every possible confidence in Mr Strang, leaving it very much in his hands, hopeful, trusting, expecting, and thinking the matter will come to something. I would rather it were done that way than writing any letters at all.

54. *Carter:* Well, Mr Chairman, I think that is rather a nice way of putting it. On the other hand I think it is rather unfair to put the onus on Mr Strang. I feel that an official letter from this particular group sitting here would get us an official answer.

55. *Brewer:* The official answer, we know what that will be.

56. *Chairman:* Shall we put, then, that we write a letter to the Council?

Omnes: Agreed.

57. *Chairman:* Leaving it to the Secretary's discretion as to whom he shall write.

58. *Kelly:* I shall write to the Council.

59. *Chairman:* Date of next meeting?

53. *Chair to group:* Gives relevant view, also backing Strang.

54. *Carter to group:* Irrelevant, expressing warmth. Gives view and relevant counter-view to Strang's. Values: Strang must not be put in a difficult position, and it is best to use official channels.

55. *Brewer to group:* Irrelevant hostile expression (to Council).

56. *Chair to group:* Makes relevant proposal, and secures general agreement.

57. *Chair to group:* Continues relevant proposal.

58. *Kelly to group:* Gives relevant information.

The course of this meeting is quite clear. A number of men, united by common irritation at the action of another organization, meet and endeavour to work out a scheme of opposition. They cast about for a definite task, but little forethought has gone into their meeting. It is noteworthy how extraordinarily large the number of views expressed is, when compared to the information exchanged. There is in fact very little developed argument: the members just move from one expressed view to another. But no particular proposal can get the support of all the members.

In the growing discomfort induced by this frustration, they find a focus of common agreement in their hostility to Strang, who represents to them the organization to which they are opposed. The strength of their feelings, which had been partly responsible for their inability to attend single-mindedly to the business of the meeting, finds an outlet in the scapegoating of Strang. When they have all expressed their emotions to their own satisfaction, they are ready to consider their task in a more business-like way. The very next proposal manages to gain their support.

The scapegoating having served its purpose, and a decision having been reached, the members are able to 'make it up to' Strang and the meeting ends in good feeling.

12

ROLE-PLAYING AS AN AID TO CLARIFICATION

Role-playing is a technique which allows members of a group to use interaction process analysis to reconsider the issues involved in common problems. Clarification is due to the explicit demonstration and analysis of the facts and values which govern the behaviour of people in interaction

ALL the previous chapters were written in such a way that the isolated student, sitting perhaps in an armchair, could learn about interaction simply by reading and introspection. Clearly, however, a time must come when he learns about social inter-action by interacting socially. It is, therefore, the aim of these concluding chapters to provide some training in the ability not only to observe critically, but also to act appropriately in a variety of settings.

How is this to be achieved? Normally, conversation goes so fast that it is difficult to learn from it while it is going on. The interaction-sequence must somehow be slowed down to allow time for analysis. It is also difficult to find a situation in which people are prepared to participate more or less naturally, while yet willing to submit their participation to critical examination. A third difficulty is that we need a group. This last problem the reader must solve for himself. Ideally, he should find some like-minded friends willing to practise their social skills. Such a group needs an organizer or chairman, whose function would be to select the situations in which the skills are to be practised, or to lead the discussion from which such a selection could emerge. It would also be his function to introduce and terminate the practice-sequences, and to keep order in the discussion following on the presentation of each sequence. The leadership might be rotated from meeting to meeting, so that every member has an opportunity to try his hand at it.

The other two difficulties can be overcome by means of the technique called 'role-playing'. In previous chapters the roles —both constructive and disruptive—which could be observed in a group, were identified and related to a variety of social circumstances. These roles, it will be remembered, were defined less in terms of personality-variables than in terms of the functions of certain kinds of contributions to the task: how these functions affected, and were affected by, the performance and expectations of others; how they affected the decisions that were made. But role-theory is not just a convenient way of classifying interpersonal behaviour. It gives insight into the function of others in the group even when one differs from them and might act differently in their place. We understand their role well enough to be able to play it if necessary.

We now meet an unfortunate confusion in terminology about which nothing can be done. In previous chapters the term 'role-playing' was used for the unconscious and natural performance of congenial roles. This usage is general in the literature. In the following chapters 'role-playing' will mean the deliberate taking over of a role which might not otherwise have been assumed. When this is done in a normal situation, for instance in a committee when the chairman is in some way inadequate, this deliberate taking over is often called 'role-taking'. This would be a useful term for the behaviour which is now to be discussed, but since it is not used in the literature concerned with artificial situations, it would probably only aggravate the confusion.

Role-playing techniques owe an immense debt to J. L. Moreno, who provided much of the original impetus for this kind of work. He was already using such techniques in Vienna in 1924, as a means of developing spontaneity of expression in a more or less psychiatric setting. He subsequently went to the United States, where he gained many adherents and influenced a large number of psychologists who have, in the course of time, diverged from Moreno's theoretical views. The divergence partly accounts for the existence now of two somewhat different techniques with two somewhat different theories behind them, Moreno and his closer associates employing 'socio-drama', and the others 'role-playing'.

In its simplest form, a role-playing situation is set up by choosing a common problem and placing oneself as a participant in the problem-situation. This may be done for a variety of reasons: to clarify the issues at stake in the situation; to train people to perform more efficiently; and, in a psychiatric setting, to enable the patient to relive, at a conscious level, an experience that is worrying him and impairing his capacity for normal living. In the psychiatric setting, self-expression, clarification, and training in performance are all involved.

The present chapter is intended to illustrate the use of role-playing in clarifying issues and clearing up confusions in people's minds. The suitability of role-playing for clarificatory purposes arises from a peculiarity which cropped up several times in the theoretical chapters: that close-knit groups tend to create for themselves a 'social reality', where ideas are expressed not because they have been verified, but because they are confirmed in conversation with other members of the group and one would look peculiar if one questioned them. If people are asked what problems are involved in living in a multi-racial community, or in firing an unsatisfactory employee, or in selecting a candidate for a job, they tend to answer in terms of the ideas current in their group. Role-playing provides a means of verification. When *talking* about problems people use the clichés of their group. But because they have participated in these problems in real life, there is a sense in which they know more than they seem to do when they talk. If they get up and *enact* a typical problem-situation, a surprising amount of material, that would never have been brought up in a discussion-group, is presented.

Clarificatory role-playing presents 'views-in-action'. The participants have an opportunity to see more clearly what facts and what values have a bearing on the situation. Since views have proposals for action implied in them, the participants will see more clearly the direction in which their views are leading them. Finally, role-playing is illuminating because it affords an opportunity for empathy. The views of others are experienced only from the outside. What is it like to know only *their* facts, have only *their* values? It is hard not to attribute moral turpitude or criminal folly to those who desire to act on principles which differ from one's own. In normal groups the presence of such differences makes for strong feeling. In a role-playing group it is possible to stand in other people's shoes for a while. This can be more illuminating than a dozen sermons.

Although, as we shall show in subsequent chapters, role-playing has a variety of uses, clarification is a good way of introducing a group to the technique, because it can be done with less self-involvement and self-criticism than the others require. When a group is unaccustomed to this kind of work it is best to start with a clear problem with which the members are already familiar. This allows for 'warming-up' by giving the untutored imagination something to cling to. The example which follows may, for instance, be read as a play, with two actors and a commentator. Everyone in the group should have a copy to allow him to follow the text without difficulty.

Trouble in the Canteen

Mr Armstrong, Works Manager of Accessories Ltd, sat at lunch in the Senior Staff Canteen next to his colleague and friend Mr Marshall, the firm's Education Officer. It was obvious to Mr Marshall that Mr Armstrong was having one of his 'off days'.

Marshall: Things not running to schedule?

Armstrong: Do they ever in this place? What with the rising cost of overheads, the Board expecting me to have my finger on every little thing, and having to be a wet-nurse to the whole organization, it's enough to upset any man! And it isn't as though I can go home and forget it all, either.

I don't know whether this job is worth it after all. I had far greater peace of mind when I worked on the bench.

Marshall: But surely you can relax when you get home?

Armstrong: Relax! Relax, with this stupid inefficient educational system we've got today! (*Takes several deep breaths.*) I saw my boy's headmaster yesterday and asked him how the lad was getting on. He works hard enough, it appears, but might not have the capacity to be selected for a Grammar School. Hasn't 'the capacity' be damned! If his teachers got down to their jobs of *teaching* instead of fooling around with free milk, savings stamps, and all these other idiotic ideas, I wouldn't have to spend my evenings trying to coach him. The wife isn't much help either. She says she just wants him to be happy. As though he could be in some unimportant little job!

I came up to this position the hard way, worked my way up step by step. Those days are gone. All your apprentices have had Grammar School education and in future the top men will be selected from them and from those who come to us from the universities. And a bright lot *they* are, with their fancy theories! I would give anything to see my boy up there on top! I'm going to give him the best possible start in life and that means he must get to Grammar School. So there you are, evening after evening I've got to do his teachers' work!

Marshall: Perhaps your boy is better equipped for some other work. (*Mr Armstrong's look was sufficient to make Mr Marshall change the subject.*)

Marshall: Overhead rates going up again?

Armstrong: Yes. And mostly through sheer inefficiency of the supervision. When I was a foreman, I knew what my men were doing all the time. It strikes me that foremen nowadays want to spend their time in an office and either won't or can't show the men just how a job can be done.

Marshall: Do you think that the bonus system has to some degree replaced the necessity of supervision? I mean, a fellow will work hard enough if he knows that it will put more money in his wage packet.

Armstrong: There is some truth in that, but only when the orders are large enough and there is a continuity of work. But it is with these small jobs that the trouble starts. Take the case I had to handle this morning. The Special Freight Carriers want to move the hinge points on a door in one of their special tanks. It was estimated that the job should take twenty hours and we agreed with the company to supply them for £25.

Well, this morning the Costs Manager brought to my notice that these packings had cost £65 to produce; £40 over the estimated price! I can tell you I was out there on the shop floor to find out why! Lack of proper supervision. That's what it was. I told that foreman some truths, I can tell you. I asked him: 'How did you manage to spend three days making eight packings?' He said: 'Mr Armstrong, I always do as good a job as I can on every job that I do.' I can't deny that either. But why in heaven's name can't people see that we can't afford to make gold-plated jobs?

Anyway, I think these chaps in the shop won't exert themselves to earn a good bonus when the guaranteed bonus is so satisfactory. Do you know, Mr Marshall, that I suspect that some of the time that chap spent on that job was spent on doing a job for himself? I know he's got a caravan and I've got a suspicion that quite a number of the parts are made in here.

Marshall: Well, the returning-to-work bell has gone long ago. We'd better be going.

Armstrong: What's a quarter of an hour? What's the good of being an executive if we can't enjoy these little privileges?

This could be followed by a discussion around the following questions:

1. What are Mr Armstrong's attitudes to other people and their work?

2. What would you have done if you had been the foreman
    a. when he received the order
    b. when he discovered what had happened?

3. What was the attitude of the senior workman who had been given the job
    a. to his work
    b. to the group and the firm
    c. to reward?

4. In what way could or should what happened have been avoided? By whom? If you had been in his shoes, what would you have done?

Such questions may naturally lead to role-playing on one of the issues, and it would be especially interesting to have someone who had defended the foreman in Armstrong's position, and a man who agreed with Armstrong playing the foreman. Another example, from Lippitt's *Training in Community Relations* will show what may happen then.

The first step in role-playing

A group of American administrators and social workers is discussing club-work. One of the members has just said: 'With the attitudes the way they are, it's almost impossible to get the children to come together for any kind of play-activity.' The discussion-leader sees this as a characteristic expression of hopelessness when confronted with a task at which everyone seems to have failed. He takes it up and after some more discussion, delegate 4 and delegate 8 sketch quickly the setting just after school, with delegate 8 playing his own role in real life, and delegate 4 playing the role of a negro girl of about thirteen years.

Leader: Fine, now let's see what happens.
Adult Worker: Hi, Nancy, I haven't seen you around lately. I suppose school's keeping you pretty busy?
Nancy: Uhhuh.

Adult Worker: Did you know we have a group every Wednesday night now, Nancy, for singing and folk-dancing and dancing games?

Nancy: Yeah, I heard something about it.

Adult Worker: Well, I know how much you like to sing and dance, Nancy. Why don't you come over tomorrow night and see if it isn't a lot of fun?

Nancy: Well, I don't think I can come. I got a lot of work. . . . It sure would be fun, I guess. (*Pause.*) What other kids come?

Adult Worker names several.

Nancy: I guess none of them are from around my house. I guess it's kids I wouldn't know.

Adult Worker: Well, couldn't you get several of your friends to come along with you?

Nancy: Well, I guess they'd say they wouldn't want to come along because they'd say they wouldn't know anybody, and it's not really their gang.

(The conversation continues for another minute or so with Nancy giving various other evidence of her perception that she and her friends would be rejected in the Wednesday evening group, and asking the worker if it might not be possible to start another singing and dancing group for 'her gang' on some other night. The leader finally cuts the scene.)

Leader: Well, does that give us a fair sample of what typically goes on?

(A number of delegates nod. Everyone has been completely engrossed in the episode.)

Leader (*to delegate 4*): Was that a pretty valid picture of the way it happens?

Delegate 4: Yes, she (*delegate 8*) did a swell job. I've had conversation like that dozens of times.

Leader (*going to blackboard*)*:* Let's list now some of your hunches as to why Nancy was feeling and acting the way she was, and where we need to look further to get a clear understanding of the problem.

Delegate 11: I got a feeling Nancy didn't think the adult worker really wanted her to come.

Delegate 13: And she really saw herself standing around on one foot and then the other and not finding any way to get in if she did go Wednesday night.

From such discussions, ways and means of improving the situation have a chance of being more thoroughly and relevantly examined.

BIBLIOGRAPHY

Moreno J. L., *Who Shall Survive?*, op. cit.

Watson G. (ed.), *Civilian Morale*, op. cit. (ch. 12 by A. Bavelas)

Hoslett S. D., *Human Factors in Management* (Park College Press, Miss., 1946).

Klapman J. W., *Group Psychotherapy*, op. cit.

J. Social Issues (1948), a whole issue is devoted to discussion-techniques in vol. IV.

Bierer J. (ed.), *Therapeutic Social Clubs*, op. cit.

Lippitt R., *Training in Community Relations*, op. cit.

Slavson S. R., *Analytic Group Psychotherapy*, op. cit.

Sociometry (1951), a whole issue is devoted to socio-drama in vol. XIV.

Maier N. R. F., *Principles of Human Relations* (Wiley, New York, 1952).

Thelen H. A., *Dynamics of Groups at Work*, op. cit.

Corsini R. J., *Methods of Group Psychotherapy*, op. cit.

13

ROLE-PLAYING AS A TRAINING-DEVICE

Clarification leads to a better understanding of the roles which require to be performed in difficult situations. Role-playing gives an opportunity to practise the roles which are required in these situations but which tend to be performed inadequately because they are not naturally congenial.

WITH an inexperienced group it is always desirable to start a role-playing session with a sequence which is mainly clarificatory. This allays anxieties about personal inadequacies and allows spontaneity to develop. It is odd but true that, once a group has got going, the members enjoy themselves so much that almost imperceptibly they move over to a discussion of improved techniques for the better performance of the required roles. Indeed, it is often difficult to keep them off using the group as a training-device when the purpose of the session is mainly clarificatory. But that is once they have started. Initially there is some reluctance to be overcome and this is best done by insisting on the impersonal, clarificatory purpose of the session.

In order to facilitate the transition from clarification to training, a sequence like the last chapter's *Trouble in the Canteen* can be used to introduce a situation in which a man 'like Mr Armstrong' has to perform a task resembling that for which training is intended. It can then be stressed that there need be no reluctance to participate because the members are asked to play roles which someone else might play naturally, and not necessarily ones which they themselves would play or that they find congenial. Criticism can then be directed at the effect that a given role has on the performance of a given task, and not at the personality of the member who happens to be playing that role. It should be clear that playing a role is not the same as acting a part in a play. Anyone can play a role: if one is awkward at it, one merely sets the other participants the additional problem of dealing with an odd, unpredictable, or inarticulate person in that situation.

The third stage comes when a new role has to be learnt, or present behaviour modified in some way. Some people are more or less unaware of the effect of their own behaviour on that of others, and thus unaware of a possible need for improvement. They know what role they intend to enact, but do not realize that all sorts of circumstances affect other people's reception of their contribution. Because of the rational and conscious level at which the argument is pursued in this book, we must leave out of consideration those people who get on badly in groups because of deep-seated personality defects. Many people function unsatisfactorily in groups simply because of superficial bad habits acquired over years of interaction without reflection or forethought. These bad habits have a chance of being corrected in the course of role-playing because their effect can be demonstrated in practice and discussed. To play a role, or see a role played, is often very illuminating to one's own routine behaviour and decisions. As in the therapeutic group, an opportunity is provided to stop and think about situations which are so familiar that they are never consciously evaluated. Unless this opportunity is given one may never be faced explicitly with either the need, or the means, of improvement.

The general principle underlying the technique is, therefore, that an artificially permissive environment is created, which makes insight and subsequent efforts at improvement possible. In the examples which follow, post-graduate students in social work are being trained for a professional role which will later have to be played in the less permissive, more censorious everyday world. Both clarification and training are involved. All the examples come from a sequence with the same group, which had started off with a reading of *Trouble in the Canteen*.

Defining the role 'Mr Armstrong'

Leader: Jolly good. Very nicely done. Well now, what sort of chap is Mr Armstrong?

Member of the group: Typical self-made man.

Leader: Uhhuh . . . (*pause*) . . . he's a typical self-made man. Go on. There's a lot to be said about him. . . . What sort of character has he got?

Another member: Rather selfish.

Leader: Rather selfish.

A member: Well, he's got the sort of personality that he can't really understand anyone else.

Leader: Yes . . . yes?

A member: He's got all the drive which has made him get on, without noticing others.

Leader: And that makes him appear selfish—no, it makes him *be* selfish . . . more?

A member: . . . (inaudible) . . .

Leader: He what?

Same member: He rather contradicts himself.

Leader: He rather contradicts himself.

Same member: About being a self-made man and the schooling.

Another member: And about the work.

Another member: Yes. (*Everyone laughs.*)

Another member: He's not very clever. (*More laughter.*)

Another member: But very pig-headed. (*More laughter.*)

Leader: Well, now we know the kind of thing this kind of person does. Now let us introduce a new character and a new situation.

The next sequence can be played without a script. Let both the actors be 'Mr Armstrong' types of characters. Suppose that the group decides to have a new situation in which Mr Armstrong has gone to see the headmaster about his boy's schooling. The leader introduces them.

Playing the role 'Mr Armstrong'

Leader: Well now, you've knocked at this headmaster's study door. You're going to go in and say good morning. Off you go.

Armstrong: Good morning. My boy, you know my boy . . . Tommy (*everyone laughs*) . . . in the third form.

Headmaster: Yes, quite well. (*More laughter.*)

Armstrong: Although he has gained in general quite well, you say, the teacher now says he hasn't the capacity to get into Grammar School. Now we can't understand this at all.

Headmaster: Yes, Mr Armstrong, I remember taking the report myself, on that. We just don't think he's the capacity to get into Grammar School and we have judged by educational tests that this is so.

Armstrong: Ah, but he'll never amount to anything unless he goes to Grammar School first. You've no right to have the responsibility of judging what he's cut out for.

Headmaster: I think I am the best judge of that, Mr Armstrong. We here can judge from his work what he's cut out for.

Armstrong: Ah, but surely we know better about it than you who only see him for a few hours in the day.

Headmaster: I can't agree with you at all about that. I am sure it is not unfair at all. We see him; he's a very good chance here.

Headmaster: You must see . . .
Armstrong: But need you . . . } *together.*

Leader: Thank you. Now let us listen to it again.

(*The recording is then played back.*)

In the case here quoted the group laughs a good deal, recognizing the many ways in which this discussion is patently ineffective and acrimonious. They even use such terms as 'expressive behaviour' to explain why Armstrong and the headmaster remained at cross-purposes.

A new situation, further removed from the introductory *Trouble in the Canteen*, can now be introduced. The group decides that a headmaster is to tell a parent that his child should go to a special school for educationally subnormal children. The actors are allowed to assume any personality they like. To make things easier for the actors, the leader may elicit from the group some of the points that would arise in such a discussion before they start: the boy's future, the family's embarrassment and so on. Once again the leader sets the scene:

Role-playing as a training-device

Leader: You're in the room. Say good morning and you're off.

1. *King:* Good morning, Mr Parr.

2. *Parr:* Good morning, Mr King.

3. *King:* I understand you want to speak to me about Johnnie, is that right?

4. *Parr:* Yes, sir.

5. *King:* Well, Mr Parr, I am glad you've called because I am sure this is a subject on which it would be as well to have a chat. Now . . . Johnnie . . . we've decided, as I think I've told you, that it would be better for him if he went to a Special School. Now on hearing that, what do you first feel about it? I'd like to hear a little of how you feel about it first.

6. *Parr:* My wife and I are a little worried about this. We don't quite understand what is meant by a special school, but presumably it means that Johnnie is not quite as bright as he should be. Is that right?

7. *King:* Well . . . er . . . I thought that that's the . . . er
. . . impression that goes about and I thought I'd
like to . . . er . . . clarify it. It's putting it a bit too
simply really to say that he's not as bright as the
others . . . er . . . no doubt he's got a lot of potentialities
but . . . er . . . as you'll appreciate . . . er . . . certain
children respond to different ways of teaching . . . er
. . . and it's been decided . . . mind you, I must say
before I really go into the argument that we've come
to this conclusion after a great deal of talking among
ourselves, that is the teachers, and that . . . er . . . the
school to which we want to send him is a type . . . er
. . . where the boys go who are such that they can't
respond to the teaching, well, the teaching that we
can give them here. Does that help at all?

8. *Parr:* What I don't understand, Mr King, is how all this
came out. Surely Johnnie has been well treated at
home, well looked after, there's nothing wrong with
our way of bringing him up. How on earth does this
situation come about?

9. *King:* No, it's nothing to do with the home background
at all. I am sure, Mr Parr, that you and your wife
have done everything for him . . . er . . . it's come to
light during the course of teaching at school . . . er . . .
naturally we assess by reports, we judge by the progress
and by the general response; we know how they're
progressing, you see, and he's been progressing in a way
we don't like to see and that's why we think a change
of school would be a good idea for him, you see.

10. *Parr:* But this special school, won't that mean he'll be
branded for life so that when he leaves it he won't be
able to get a decent job? That's the sort of thing that's
involved, isn't it?

11. *King:* No, he won't necessarily be branded, in fact he
won't be branded at all. Goodness knows there are
a lot of people now who go to these schools and they
get perfectly good jobs afterwards. You see, it's really

a different type of education. He certainly won't be branded at all.

12. *Parr:* But what about the neighbours? We come from a good neighbourhood, you know. And I've heard it spoken of by my neighbours as a most degrading thing that a person should go to a special school, and is it absolutely necessary?

13. *King:* Well, Mr Parr, I am sure you won't make a decision on just what the neighbours think, because they don't know the whole story behind these schools. They've got the whole idea of it wrong. There is surely no disgrace in being sent to another school because he can't settle down at the one he's at. I am sure you won't place undue deference to what other people think, who know nothing about it at all.

14. *Parr:* No, of course, we're only thinking of his welfare and we do see if it's necessary he must go to this . . . this . . .

15. *King:* Well, Mr Parr, I must assure you, you see, that this decision we've come to is being taken purely on the very same grounds of his welfare. We want to see the best thing done for him and it has been decided that the very best thing is to go to this school and therefore a change of school is really necessary for him. I hope . . . I hope . . . that you and your wife will see that and see that it is not degrading but just the thing that is the best possible thing for the child himself.

16. *Parr:* And what will happen when he leaves? Can you tell me that? What about exams and so forth and so on? How will he be placed, being in this special school?

17. *King:* Well, as regards academic examinations . . . er . . . it all depends on how he progresses in his various subjects, but the type of job which he will get need not necessarily demand any qualifications of an academic standard. No doubt his interests while he's at the school will become obvious and we shall find that we shall succeed because there are so many openings

nowadays, good openings too, in fitting him for a job that he's interested in.

18. *Parr:* He won't have to go away from home for this, will he? (*They look at the instructor for guidance. She says 'As you please.'*)

19. *King:* No, that need not necessarily be so. The school we have in mind is not far away from the neighbourhood in which he lives.

20. *Parr:* I see, and could you tell me, please, whether my wife and I can do anything further to help him? Suppose that we go on a bit further, is there anything we can do to boost his schooling?

21. *King:* Well, I am sure you and your wife have been doing all you can for him. It's obvious from meeting you that you are the kind of parent that has his child's welfare at heart and all I can ask you to do is to keep on showing the affection and kindliness that you have been showing, and should he ask for any help, well, I'm sure you'll be only too glad to give it to him, and if you do that, that'll be very good.

22. *Parr:* I'm very grateful to you, Mr King, for your help and for the kindly way in which you've explained matters, and I'll be able to tell my wife now just exactly why he's being sent there.

23. *King:* I'm only too pleased to help you in any way I can and I hope that you will realize that it is for his welfare entirely that we think he should go to this school.

24. *Parr:* Thank you very much . . .

   Leader: And thank you very much. That was fine.

This sequence, which was recorded, was then played back to the group several times. (An alternative method is to have the conversation taken down in shorthand and duplicated for the next session.) The following points emerged from the discussion.

5. King gives his decision first. Then he asks Parr how he

feels about it. King has obviously been told once upon a time that you must ask people how they feel about things, but what is the point of announcing a decision first and then asking for reaction? It is only prying.

6. Parr behaves very much as an interviewer in 'In Town Tonight'. He does not seem to react like a real, concerned parent at all.

7. Some students feel that King is here wrapping things up too much. There is some discussion on this.

11. King behaves in an agitated, fussy sort of way. 'Won't necessarily be branded . . . won't be branded at all . . . certainly won't be branded at all'—as though he is trying to convince himself.

13. King impatiently slaps him down.

14. Parr duly retreats, but one may ask oneself how far is he really being reassured by King's manner.

15. King does not leave Parr time either to explain himself or to get used to the idea by thinking aloud. He is too anxious to keep control over what will be said. This contribution is really a lengthy assertion with stress on the fact that the decision is not Parr's but King's.

16. Perhaps Parr's frequent change of topic (see also contribution 18) is due to the fact that he feels no real assurance forthcoming from King. The question about exams seems to show that Parr has as yet no real notion of what is involved.

17. No wonder King is hard put to it to gloss this over.

22. It is quite untrue that Parr now knows more about Johnnie than he did at the beginning of the interview. And if Mrs Parr is a woman of sense and character, he will undoubtedly discover that he knows no more now. Then presumably there will be a second interview with the headmaster. It is also noticed that King has frequently used the expression 'sent to this school' and Parr is now taking it over.

In general the group comments that Parr is too easy-going and does not present King with any difficulties. They are beginning to want to see the fur fly. The comment on King is 'a typical schoolmaster', not accustomed to listening to what is being said to him. (The members of the group are just beginning to learn to do this.) He is called woolly, involved, authoritarian. His frequent use of the phrase 'not necessarily' arouses unfavourable comment.

When all this has been sorted out, the instructor has three choices before him. He can change the function of the role-playing session and give the members an opportunity to discuss shortcomings in their interaction techniques. They are here reacting with some intolerance to tendencies of their own which they see externalized and consciously perhaps for the first time. This kind of learning can also be done explicitly later, or one may hope that with practice the lesson will just quietly sink in. Or, secondly, the session may turn into a clarificatory discussion on what is involved for a parent adjusting himself to the idea that his child is educationally subnormal. Or, thirdly, the group may go on with the role-playing practice. A discussion may develop on how the headmaster might have been more likable and helped Mr Parr more. In that case the group reverts to earlier lessons on the sequence of decision-making. First ask for and give information; then ask for views and make suggestions and plans; then see if agreement can be secured. The group which is used as an example here wants to do this, and now goes through the situation again, paying special attention to the sequence of decision-making. The headmaster gives the information first.

Headmaster: We've been following his progress during this time. . . . We found that on occasion he's slipped up a bit, although he's shown great initiative and interest in sports, and his carpentry is very good, and we thought . . . I've spoken to his other teacher and we're not sure he would not be happier in a Special School, where the standards are different from our own, in some things not quite so high, and they spend more time on handwork. I'm wondering if you could perhaps throw light on the subject from the home point of view.

Parent: Yes, well, my husband and I have been rather worried over this. We've noticed he doesn't really seem very happy at school and that he wasn't going on as he might. . . .

This time the headmaster takes pains to give the parent ample opportunity to get used to the information, shows possible solutions, and gives the parent time to sort herself out before she begins to feel that a particular decision might be a good one. The listening group sees that this process must never be hurried and that it may be necessary to go back several times to the beginning and give further information, e.g.:

Parent: Yes, that sounds very interesting. We'd like to know more about that. My husband and I . . . (*tails off*).

Headmaster: I wonder if you would like to go and see that school? I could easily arrange it.

Two things are happening in this group. The members are practising skills which they will later use in their professional life; and they are now coming to the stage where group self-evaluation is obviously the next thing they will want to do.

14

ROLE-PLAYING AND GROUP
SELF-EVALUATION

*The final stage is: to participate in the making of decisions
while remaining aware of the structure of the task, of the structure of the group, and of one's own impact upon both. The step
before this final stage is to split these requirements into participation on the one hand, and observation on the other.*

IN THE previous chapter it was shown that people can be
made aware of the effect of what they are saying on someone
else; and can be made to modify their behaviour accordingly.
This is not so very difficult in a conversation in which only
two people take part. The next step is, however, harder to
take. The same sense of knowing what is going on must now
be developed in a much larger group. Three things are involved simultaneously: thinking in terms of the task, thinking
in terms of the effect one's behaviour has on others, thinking
in terms of the effect other members have on each other. None
of these three kinds of awareness ought to be developed at the
expense of the other two; one should be able to keep track of
all three aspects while the group is actually doing its job. But
it requires training and discipline to be perceptive at three
levels simultaneously.

Eventually, a group that is seeking to improve its proficiency will have to learn to recognize these ways of behaviour
without conscious attention or reflection, since proficiency is
not served when people are so preoccupied with analysis that
they do not participate in making the decision. For the purpose
of training, however, one may start by appointing group-
observers who take no part in the discussion, but who perform
the functions which all members will eventually have to add
to what they are already doing.

The group is, therefore, divided into participants and observers. The participants are instructed to consider themselves as a committee, to select a problem for discussion, and if necessary to allot to each member a social setting by which his ideas are to be affected or an organization which has delegated to him the representation of its views and interests. (Time has to be allowed for them to think this out in detail, and in practice it is therefore best to make preliminary arrangements at the end of a preceding session. As a rule, the participants will find it useful to have an informal meeting of their own, at which the instructor need not be present, to work out a rough plan.)

The observer's task is to note the participants' contributions in the schedule given below:

| From Whom? | To Whom? | Task related | | | | | | | Expressive | | | Content-reminder |
		inf +	inf –	vi +	vi –	(pro)	agr+	agr–	f	h	w	
:	:	:	:	:	:	:	:	:	:	:	:	:

The schedule allows a column per interaction-category, so that a tick can mark the type of contribution made. At times it is convenient to have a note of explicit proposals, and this may be allowed a place on the schedule when occasion demands it. The difference between implied and open contributions in the agreement-category is most easily marked by entering, instead of a tick, 'i' or 'o' as appropriate. Space is also given for brief notes on what is actually taking place, e.g. to note a change in topic, necessary and unnecessary flannelling, etc.

The whole group will want to discuss the observers' findings at the end of the sequence. For this purpose it is worth while to go through a recording of the sequence in conjunction with the observers' reports. Each member can then be asked what he was doing:

Analysis from participants' self-evaluation

I am (or he is) contributing to interaction-category . . .

if information: exploring ideas already expressed?
or introducing new facts?

if views: what values and what facts?
had they already been taken into account?
or introducing new ideas?

if agreement: I am supporting member x (or not)
he is supporting me (or not)

if expressive: this was purely self-expressive
this was consciously cohesive in intention

Members may also be able to answer from introspection:
I am getting the response I expected
or the response I expected was . . .

If this discussion is left until the next meeting of the group, the observers will have had time to make a further analysis from their interaction-schedule. This analysis uses compound categories constructed from the simpler ones.

Later analysis from the observers' interaction-schedule

A. The social context of the group: an analysis of the external affiliations of the members.

B. (where appropriate) Was problem-definition or procedural discussion necessary and adequate? (If this question arises, the relevant parts of section C may be used.)

C. Description of the task and the internal structure of the group.

Information:

1. a. What information was necessary for good performance?

   b. Was all the necessary information provided?
      If there were gaps in the information, were members
      aware of it?

   c. Who were the information-givers (experts)? (This may
      be obtained from the categories inf+ and vi+ with
      large factual content.)

2. a. How much facilitation was necessary for good per-
      formance?

   b. Who were the facilitators? (From inf— and vi—.)

   c. Which members in particular benefited from the facili-
      tators? (From inf+ and vi+ after inf— and vi—.)

   d. Were all available talents exploited? (From affiliations,
      content-reminders, inf+ and vi+.)

Views:

3. a. How much co-ordination and direction was necessary?

   b. Who were the co-ordinators? (From vi+ and pro.)

   c. Did anyone specialize in making explicit proposals?

   d. How successful was each co-ordinator? (From agree-
      ment-category following views and proposals, with a
      glance at content-reminders.)

   e. Were all views taken into consideration? (From vi+
      and content-reminder— and ask them!)

4. a. Who were the value-asserters? (From vi+ with a large
      value component.)

   b. Who were the opinion-leaders? (From vi+ and inf+
      when followed by agreement.)

   c. Who was a supporter? Of whom?

   d. Who changed his mind? (From content-reminders with
      reference to group affiliations.)
      Was there in general much unfreezing of attitudes?

The expressive area:

5. a. How much morale-maintenance was necessary?
   b. Who was withdrawn? (From interaction-category 'w' and total contribution score.)
   c. Who was hostile? To whom?
   d. Who was friendly? To whom?

From this analysis, the worker with small groups will find it possible to answer without difficulty such wide questions as: Was the group too dependent on anyone? Were functions well distributed among the members? Was the group sufficiently task-related?

There follows now a 'case-conference' produced by five students with social-work training. They had been asked to construct a case in which different members possessed different sets of information, with different affiliations, from which a conflict of values might arise. A recording of their session was played back to them and their observers. At the end of the playback, some of the questions raised in the previous paragraphs were discussed. The remarks on the right-hand side of the verbatim record, which is given below, were among those elicited during this discussion.

CASE CONFERENCE

1. *Chairman:* Good morning, ladies and gentlemen. I am not sure if you all know each other, so I will introduce you for a start. Mr Ryland-Hulme is a Superintendent of the Remand Home, Mr Carson one of the Child Care Officers, Miss Smith, who is a teacher at the Secondary Modern School, and Miss Perry, who is one of the Probation Officers. Well, we are here this morning to discuss the case of John Brown, who is at present in the Remand Home. Perhaps, Mr Carson, you would like to put the facts of the case before the meeting.

2. *Mr Carson:* Well, John has been known to the Department for a number of years because we have been working with the family from the point of view of preventive work. He has, as you probably know, been on probation and he has just broken it. The home itself is in many ways unsatisfactory, and there is certainly not much discipline . . . but I think my Department feels that it would be a shame to break that family up. I don't think I can say any more at the moment.

3. *Chairman:* I think that John Brown is at present on a fortnight's remand on a charge of breaking and entering—is it, Mr Carson—with larceny?

4. *Mr Carson:* Yes.

5. *Chairman:* How has John been in the Remand Home?

6. *Mr Ryland-Hulme:* Well, John has been with us for just over a fortnight now. I should say in the first week he showed a suspicious, surly attitude. He preferred his own company to that of the other boys. Gradually he began to show his superior intelligence and perhaps also strength of character by influencing the other children, and he was responsible for several outbursts against authority which took place, especially in the evenings when my housemaster was attempting to organize the children's activities.

1. 'I am giving information, which may be necessary or may be necessary flannelling.'
No other comments.

2. 'I am giving the information asked for. I am proposing that he should not be removed from his family.'
This proposal involves the value that a family should not be broken up.

3.
5. } 'I am still getting all the relevant information together.'

4. 'I am giving the information.'

6. 'I am giving the information asked for. I had all this written out beforehand in case I should be asked.'

7. *Miss Smith:* It sounds like the same John.

8. *Mr Ryland-Hulme:* His attitude towards the staff showed aggression. He refused to do his duties, such as making his bed, but despite this, he on several occasions approached the house-parent, showing an attempt to strike up a relationship with him. I should say he is an emotionally disturbed child. . . . I suggest that he is an extremely insecure maladjusted child, which has possibly been brought about by the difficult parental relationships which I don't think were fully mentioned by Mr Carson, the Child Care Officer. I suggest there is a need for him to fulfil his intellectual potentialities and I suggest that this can be best brought about by putting him in a school for maladjusted children rather than perhaps Approved School treatment of a disciplinary type.

9. *Chairman:* Mr Ryland-Hulme mentioned the parental disharmony, Mr Carson. Would you like to say something?

10. *Mr Carson:* There is not really any parental disharmony. I mean, they are not the sort of parental relationships which Mr Ryland-Hulme is probably used to in his own circumstances, but they are probably very normal, and in stressing the intellectual angle I feel the emotional angle is far more important, and if he won't work up to his capacity, well, he just won't under any circumstances. I think it is far more important that he should have a good relationship which is there and he should keep that as much as possible.

(*Miss Perry and Mr Ryland-Hulme interrupt.*)

11. *Chairman:* You feel quite certain that there is a satisfactory relationship between John and his parents?

7. 'I don't know why I said this. I suppose one could say I was confirming the impression given by Mr Ryland-Hulme. Or was I just putting my oar in?'

8. 'I just heard Miss Smith encouraging me in the background. But I had not finished my bit of paper, so I did not take much notice.'

    'I am just giving information. I was not thinking about how Mr Carson might react to this.' (*Mr Carson:* 'I felt that Mr Ryland-Hulme had no business to make an analysis of this kind, he had only seen the boy for a fortnight. His suggestion about sending the boy away went right against what I wanted.')

    'I am proposing that John should leave home.'

    Ryland-Hulme seems to have two values: 1. Maladjustment must be dealt with by skilled treatment in a special environment. 2. Intellectual potentialities must be fulfilled. He has not considered the other value stated in the group, namely that homes should not be broken.

9. 'I just want the point cleared up.'

    He asks for information.

10. 'I am pleased to be asked to take the point up. The chairman is my superior at the office and I am expecting her to support me. I give further information. It felt all right when I was saying it, but I see now that it is rather vague.'

    He is, of course, proposing that his values should govern the decision.

    (*Mr Ryland-Hulme:* 'He is not really meeting my point at all, but just makes assertions.')

    (*Miss Perry:* 'I think I wanted to say what I did say a little later on.')

11. 'I asked the question which I thought the others wanted to know about.'

12. *Mr Carson:* Oh, it is definitely there. There is not a discipline, but perhaps the Probation Officer can tell us whether any outsider's discipline is of any use.

13. *Chairman:* Miss Perry?

14. *Miss Perry:* There is a relationship prevalent in the home and we saw how fond the mother was of the child in the Court. But whether that is a helpful relationship, I don't know. I would not like to agree. John is an intelligent child, as we have been hearing. He has had an I.Q. test since he has been in the Remand Home, has he?

15. *Mr Ryland-Hulme:* Yes, that has been done. His I.Q. is 130, which is far above that of either of his parents. In view of the extremely lax attitude of his father, who is a drunk and rarely works, I believe, he seems . . .
    (*Miss Perry interrupts.*)

16. *Miss Perry:* I don't think John is disturbed. I would agree that his father does not play any part in the home. . . .

17. *Miss Smith:* Don't you think that wherever John is, he feels the odd one out? That has always been his problem, he is more intelligent than his parents. They don't really understand him and they think that it is perfectly normal for him to be at a Secondary Modern School, whereas I think that had his early school life been different and had he been at school more regularly, he would not be in a Secondary Modern School at all, but in a Grammar School.

18. *Chairman:* Miss Smith, would you like to explain why John's attendance at school has been so poor?

19. *Miss Smith:* Well, he is just one of those children who takes an odd day off, and so he is always confused—he never knows what has been happening the week before. I don't know whether it is truancy perhaps, but it is a half-day here and half-day there. (*A number of people talk at this point.*) (*Mr Carson makes several attempts*

12. 'I am giving information, and I am hoping for confirmation from Miss Perry.'

14. 'I say what I wanted to say earlier on. I don't know what made me ask about the I.Q. Perhaps I was wanting to make an end to the wrangle between Mr Carson and Mr Ryland-Hulme. I think Carson has made up his mind what he wants and I can't support him. I have not made up my mind what I want for the boy. Perhaps I asked about the I.Q. just to get more facts to help me.'

15. 'I give the information asked for, but really I want to get back to the issue that arose before. . . . Yes, I do sound rather tied by the book, don't I?'
    (*Miss Smith:* 'I feel this question should have been answered by me.')

16. 'I am still trying to get the facts straight.'
    (*Ryland-Hulme:* 'No, I did not mind Miss Perry's interruption.')

17. 'I think it about time I was asked to contribute. I feel that these social workers don't take much notice of me. I rather blame the chairman for this.' (Several others say that they think the chairman very good.) 'I am giving information which I consider relevant, though I am not yet sure where it will lead. I am not proposing anything in particular.'

18. 'I think she rambles rather and I want to get her back to policy-problems.'

19. 'I give information, but I am not proposing anything.' 'I am a bit annoyed at the interruptions and raised my voice to be heard above Mr Carson.' (The others say they interrupted because she was so hesitant and kept repeating herself.) 'I have to do this because you are not listening to me.'

to interrupt.) It makes a lot of difference in school if they miss just one morning: then he cannot follow at the beginning of the lesson.

20. *Mr Carson:* But you have known this child for some time and observed his attitude.

21. *Chairman:* Excuse me, could I just clear up this point, please, Miss Smith? His progress at school is due to lack of supervision at home. His parents don't make the necessary effort. It is not due to any . . .

22. *Miss Smith:* No, I think he is probably encouraged to take an odd half-day off. . . .

23. *Mr Carson:* Ah, no, his parents send him out in the morning and think he is going to school and he goes instead to a gang of boys and he is definitely the leader. But all this business about the bad home, I must protest here. We have been working with this family for quite a long time and I feel we are making progress, and judging by your implications rather than by anything else, I would not like to see this boy removed from home, because I feel that it would just about ruin two years' reasonably good work by myself and two colleagues.

24. *Miss Perry:* Do you think John's progress has shown that he is improving? He is again up before the Court on a similar charge as the one before.

25. *Mr Carson:* It is quite symptomatic. I am not saying . . . It is symptomatic of his intelligence . . . I am sure the school he is attending can do something in that respect, together with work in the home.

20. 'I wish she would say that the boy could do well if he came regularly. Also I want to encourage her and get her on my side, perhaps . . . Yes, I see that I haven't gone about it very well.'

21. 'I am trying to get her to come to the point.'
    Also, if the group were to agree on the value that in-tellectual capacities must be fulfilled, and the parents are in fact a hindrance to this fulfilment, there would be a clash between this value and that a child must live with his own family. The present group of students was not sufficiently experienced to make all this explicit.

22. 'I am a bit startled at being pushed. These people think in quite different ways.'

23. Steps out of role: 'It's a bit hard to keep this up' (that is, the role the group had beforehand decided he was to play.) 'I have to keep inventing new arguments, but I felt at the time that Miss Smith was making things difficult for me when she could so easily have made them easier.'
    He is giving further information in support of his main value and proposal.

24. Also steps out of role and says to 'Mr Carson': 'But your arguments are not really very good ones. My points are quite task-related.'
    She is countering his proposal by querying the accuracy of his information.

25. 'I feel a little overwhelmed and I make my point badly, but it is a good point. If he were exercising all his faculties, including his intelligence, he would not be anti-social.' (The others say that he did not manage to convey this information and that they feel he is holding them up.

26. *Miss Smith:* But the trouble is he should not be in this school. He should really be in a Grammar School.

27. *Mr Carson:* He is not . . . He is not . . . Even his attainments are pretty poor.

28. *Miss Smith:* He could not possibly be moved to a Grammar School, but even if he can go to some other school . . .

29. *Mr Carson:* He is in a low class now, he can still go to the A-class. (*He talks about this for some time while Miss Smith makes several attempts to interrupt.*)

30. *Miss Smith:* If he can go to a different Secondary Modern School, perhaps, or I think if he can go away from his family, who will never be able to understand the academic attitude to school which he could reasonably have. But he feels that he is the odd one out.

31. *Chairman:* Miss Perry?

32. *Miss Perry:* May we know how his other brother has got on since he has been away from home? His brother was removed—sent to an Approved School two years ago.

33. *Chairman:* Excuse me, how old is his other brother?

34. *Miss Perry:* He is seventeen, and he has been in an Approved School for two years, and he will shortly be leaving school. Whether or not he will come home we are not sure yet. But he has certainly made amazing progress since he has been away from home.

35. *Mr Ryland-Hulme:* Yes, but the brother is not half as intelligent as John here.

There is some discussion on the relation between these two things; does Carson annoy them so that they do not listen to him, or does he make his points so badly that they get bored?) 'I am trying for support.'

26. 'No one is taking much notice of what I say about his school life.' On being asked what she wants them to understand . . . 'Well, I just want them to take the school into account, they keep talking about his emotions or his family.' This proposal involves her main value—that everyone should use his schooling to develop his intellectual capacities to the full.

27. 'I think here I was purely task-related. It seemed to be the logical point to make. . . . Good heavens, I was arguing against my own case.'

28. 'I do sound rather dithery.' (The others agree.)

30. 'Mr Carson is saying what I should be saying. I see now that there is no point in being annoyed at this, as long as the information is conveyed, but at the time I was vexed.' Main value restated in this proposal.

31. 'I feel that this subject is now exhausted.'

32. 'I am still trying to make up my mind and now I want to do a sort of comparison.' (*Chairman:* 'Miss Perry responds to my expectations to get away from the previous point.')

33. 'Just getting further information for the group.'

34. 'Just giving further information.'

36. *Mr Carson:* I think he is the sort of boy who would prob-
    ably get on better in the atmosphere of an Approved
    School. John here is definitely intelligent and I think he
    is beginning to appreciate the difference between him
    and his parents. . . .

37. *Miss Perry:* But are you going to get anywhere as long as
    the parents refuse to co-operate? They refuse to co-
    operate. John's been on probation for a year now . . .
    during that time . . .

38. *Chairman:* Can I just ask you what is the parents' attitude
    to this latest offence of John's? Are they making an
    effort at all to co-operate with you?

39. *Miss Perry:* I think that the father has just let it pass and
    he is not concerned about anything except himself.
    He did not come to Court. The mother is very con-
    cerned, but she is a simple soul. . . .

40. *Mr Carson:* Yes, but you Probation Officers have only
    been working with the *boy.* I am sure that it has not
    really got to the root of the problem. I am sure that
    working with the family as a complete unit we can get
    somewhere. I mean, the fact that the Probation Officers
    failed is not sufficiently indicative that he should be
    sent away.

41. *Miss Perry:* But do you feel that you can alter his mother's
    attitude? She resented the fact that he was on proba-
    tion, but did little to encourage him. . . .

42. *Mr Carson:* Yes, but . . .
    (*Both talk together.*)

43. *Chairman* (*to Carson*)*:* You feel quite strongly then that
    this boy should not be removed from home.

36. 'I feel grateful for Mr Ryland-Hulme's support and I elaborate on it.'

37. 'Both previous speakers seem to suggest that John can improve while he is at home. I feel doubtful about this. I think I am here trying to persuade the group that this would not be a good thing. I want to do this before Mr Carson and Mr Ryland-Hulme team up.'

38. 'Just clearing up a point.'

39. 'I answer the question. I had not thought about its implications. Is the chairman supporting me or not? I don't know if I am saying that the home background is bad, and so John ought to go away, or the home background is bad and the whole family must be dealt with as a unit.

40. 'I did not see these two interpretations of Miss Perry's were possible. I was so afraid that the boy would be sent away that that was the only bit I heard. I did not even realize at the time how rude I sounded to the Probation Department. What a pity I took up this antagonistic and antagonizing attitude.'

41. 'I did not actually feel it quite like that, though it does sound rude now that I hear it again. But I did definitely feel I was arguing *against* Mr Carson.'

42. ⎫ 'I see that I am still hostile to Miss Perry. I thought at the
44. ⎭ time the chairman was supporting me because she was my superior at the office.'

43. ⎫ 'I must now put a stop to this wrangle. Also time is running
45. ⎭ out and we are not coming to a conclusion. I tackle Carson first, because the others seem more capable of coming to an agreement; from here on I am trying to eliminate Carson from repeating his point uselessly.'

44. *Mr Carson:* Yes.

45. *Chairman (to Carson):* You would like to see his probation extended?

46. *Mr Carson:* Not necessarily probation, because the relationship with the Probation Officer has obviously not been particularly good, with all due respect, but if he was committed to Care, then I think we could supervise, and we could continue the supervision we have been giving quite voluntarily anyway.

47. *Miss Smith:* I don't agree. That would get you nowhere.

48. *Mr Ryland-Hulme:* I must say that committal to Care would indicate that he would be incarcerated in a children's home.

49. *Mr Carson:* Certainly not.

50. *Chairman:* You are suggesting, Mr Carson, that he should be committed to Care and supervised by the Children's Department in his own home?

51. *Mr Carson:* In his own home. It would be our own decision anyway—your decision really, but judging by the amount of work that we have done, I am sure you will agree.

52. *Chairman:* You are definitely in favour that the boy should be left at home.

53. *Mr Carson:* I am certain of it, yes.

54. *Miss Perry:* Do you think there will ever be real unity in this home? I don't see how this can be.

55. *Mr Carson:* There is unity. I mean it may not appear on the surface, but it is a sort of strong emotional unity with not very much practical sense.

56. *Mr Ryland-Hulme:* But surely you found there were frequent quarrels between the man and his wife?

57. *Mr Carson:* Well, quarrels, yes.

58. *Mr Ryland-Hulme:* Isn't it a fact that the man refuses to go to work and often comes home drunk?

47. 'I disagree with that proposal.'
48. Steps out of role. 'Sorry, I had not got the information quite right.'

49. 'That information was incorrect.'
50. 'I am clearing the point up tactfully.'

51. 'I am still reminding my boss that she *is* my boss.'

52. 'Just getting the point quite explicit, but also I wish he would make a more reasoned case out for his proposal.'
53. 'I did not realize I could say more than "yes".'
54. 'I have now made up my mind and I think Carson is wrong. I am here making an objection.'
55. 'Miss Perry is wrong.'

56. 'Mr Carson is wrong, I am supporting Miss Perry.'
    Value: children need not stay in quarrelsome homes.
57. 'I feel they don't get my point at all.'
    Value: any home is better than an institution.
58. 'I bring up further ammunition.'

59. *Mr Carson:* He comes in drunk, he doesn't work as regularly . . .

60. *Mr Ryland-Hulme:* Would you say that it is a good basis for a good home relationship?

61. *Mr Carson:* If the basic relationship is there, yes, because it is only through ignorance that the quarrels take place, and I am sure that . . .

62. *Miss Perry:* For how long have you been working with this family?

63. *Mr Carson:* Two years.

64. *Miss Perry:* And after two years, we still have John coming up before the Court with a similar charge.

65. *Mr Carson:* It is a very long-term process. But you are not going to get anywhere by cutting the family up completely.

66. *Miss Perry:* Do you think it is likely that if we leave John at home and in fact your recommendations . . . ! It makes no difference at all, we are still going to have him before the Court again in a very short time . . .

67. *Mr Carson:* No.

68. *Miss Perry:* . . . on a more serious charge.

69. *Chairman:* Miss Perry's point is probably that she has had the boy under supervision for about eighteen months.

70. *Miss Perry: It is a year now.*

59. 'I feel I am being grilled, but I knew myself to be right.'

60. 'I feel I am asking just the right questions now.'

61. 'At this point I realize that something odd is going on. Those others are judging the family in terms of morals, whereas I see it as the background of John's security. But I feel at a loss, because they ought to know better.' There is some general discussion on this, for social workers are taught it is better to judge a family according to whether the children are happy in it, and not according to whether it conforms to their view of the ideal family. They are all a little surprised at the stand they find they were taking. 'Mr Carson' at last discovers that he really had a good case to make out, which he now sees he spoiled by not making explicit earlier in the discussion the grounds on which he has come to his conclusion that this boy ought not to be sent away.

62.
64. 'I want to make two things clear. One is that we cannot
66. let the situation just go on as it is, we must make some
68. change. The other is that Mr Carson has been saying that the Probation Department has been unsuccessful. But they had John only for one year, while the Child Care people have not brought about any significant changes in two years.'

63.
65. 'I feel quite at a loss. Miss Perry ought to know you can't
67. change a problem family as easily as all that.'

69. 'I am summing up, before Miss Perry gets too awkward for
71. Mr Carson.'
    (*Mr Carson:* 'I feel she is summing up against me.')

71. *Chairman:* It is a year now he has been on Probation, and it would be simply a transfer of supervision if the boy was left at home.

72. *Mr Carson:* Well, it must have been a question of personalities.

73. *Chairman:* You are suggesting, Mr Carson, that supervision by one of the Child Care Officers . . .

74. *Mr Carson* (*interrupts*): Yes, because the boy is able to make good relationships and I think I am right in saying that he has made a very good relationship with you, Miss Smith.

75. *Miss Smith:* It does not seem to affect his school work very much. I think that if he were able to work up to his undoubted capacity he might change in his out-of-school attitude as well. He does know, I think, that he is in the wrong class at school and may even know that he shouldn't be at the school, but I don't think that he will be able to alter that and I am quite sure that no one else will, so long as he remains in the same school. I think that if he were working to capacity, his outlook would become very different from that of his family, but if you keep him in his own home with his parents, you will probably be holding him back a good deal. It would be far more difficult for him to progress as he should. If he were in an Approved School, it would have to be a carefully selected one where they had a course for the General Certificate of Education. If he could do that, I think if he were able to make relationships there, he would very, very quickly pick up the years he has lost. There would not be any of this continued absence.

76. *Chairman:* You feel, Miss Smith, that with external supervision and regular attendance, John has the ability . . .

77. *Miss Smith:* Yes, I do.

78. *Chairman:* . . . to take a distinctly higher course academically?

79. *Miss Smith:* Yes.

72. All agree this is pure expressive behaviour.

73. 'Just getting the point clear.'

74. 'I give information and also I am angling for Miss Smith's support.'

75. 'I did not realize he was angling, in fact I am still thinking of what was said much earlier in the discussion.' At this point the instructor asks the group about Miss Smith's role. She does not seem to have progressed in the discussion at all. The group says she is saying nothing of importance over and over again. Miss Smith repeats that they are taking no notice of her. They all agree that this is because she is a school-teacher and not a social worker. The instructor asks why Miss Smith was invited to the conference. Some suggest that she has information which the others lack, some suggest to secure future co-operation with the school. It is not till the instructor asks in so many words whether either of these aims is being achieved that the whole group, laughing, acknowledges that they have slipped up badly here. Miss Smith blames the chairman, who defends herself by saying it was very difficult to keep the group together.

76.
77. } 'I am trying to get the point quite clear.'

78.
79. } 'I confirm the chairman's summing up.'

80. *Mr Ryland-Hulme:* In support of Miss Smith, I should like to say that Mr Carson's argument seems to be based purely on the fact that he thinks he can do better than Miss Perry. He has inferred that he can form a better relationship than was obtained by the Probation Department.

81. *Chairman:* While we sympathize with Mr Carson, who has done a lot of very good work with this family, and who does wish to keep the family together, I think there is probably agreement that the boy does need some external discipline in which to work to a fuller capacity and that he is not getting this at home. I think we have to be realistic about this.

82. *Mr Carson:* I think if he goes to an Approved School, he will come back a criminal.

83. *Mr Ryland-Hulme:* I should like to confirm that. May I put it to you, Mr Chairman, that in the strong, essentially understanding, disciplined atmosphere which necessarily must be displayed in a Remand Home, he did not show up in a very good light, even in a fortnight? I can see that. I think that a school for maladjusted children, combined with psychiatric treatment, with perhaps an analyst, is the best . . .

84. *Miss Smith:* Is it one of these schools where he is allowed to run wild and where lessons are not organized?

85. *Mr Ryland-Hulme:* I suggest, Miss Smith, that a school for maladjusted children is merely realizing the potentialities of the child.

86. *Miss Perry:* If he goes to a classifying school, there the appropriate Approved School will be selected for John and if he needs psychiatric treatment, of course, with the classifying schools, there will be skilled people to understand his needs, and if they recommend that he needs psychiatric treatment, then he will receive it.

87. *Mr Ryland-Hulme:* Yes, that may be so.

80. 'I was only saying this as a kind of introduction to the proposal I made later on.' (*Mr Carson:* 'hostility to me'.)

81. 'I try to let down Carson as lightly as possible. I hope he will now keep quiet.' (The rest of the group noticed that this was the Chairman's intention.)

82. 'I feel I've been let down by my boss.'

83. 'This is my opening. This is what I have been aiming at throughout the discussion.'

84. Steps out of role. 'I thought this was the kind of remark a school-teacher might make.'

85. 'Just giving information' . . . but everyone laughs at this analysis.

86. 'I'm trying to get on with the job before we have a useless acrimonious discussion.'
    The proposal is that it should be recommended that Johnnie goes to a classifying school. Main value: Johnnie must be cured, and must be given an opportunity to develop his intellect to the full.

87. 'I support Miss Perry.'

88. *Chairman:* I think we have to realize here that we are making a general recommendation as to the type of discipline that the boy needs and will need, whether he is left at home or not. We are not deciding on the type of school the child will be going to.

89. *Mr Carson:* I would agree with Mr Ryland-Hulme up to a point. Do you think he could benefit by a day-school for maladjusted children where he would not necessarily have to live in?

90. *Chairman:* There would, of course, Mr Carson, be arrangements for the boy to go home on leave so the home would not be broken.

91. *Mr Ryland-Hulme:* I think the discrepancy is far too great between the home influences and the influences at school.

92. *Miss Perry:* We must remember that John is known as the leader of a gang in the district and it is going to be very difficult for him to live amongst these boys who are looking for him to carry on in his old anti-social activities if he is, in fact, going to conform more to social demands.

93. *Chairman:* Would I be voicing the opinions of this conference then in suggesting that John be removed from his home circumstances, while Mr Carson continues his very good work with the family? When suitable, the boy could return home, but meanwhile he needs stronger and firmer influences of a more disciplined environment.

94. *Miss Smith:* And fresh opportunity too.

95. *Mr Ryland-Hulme:* I would support that.

96. *Chairman:* Thank you very much indeed.

88. 'I am tactfully giving them the right information about the powers of this committee.' (The others agree that it did not antagonize them.)

89. 'I am suggesting a compromise between my view and theirs.'

90. 'Just giving information.'

91. 'I am referring to Mr Carson's proposal and disagreeing with it.'

92. 'So am I. I am supporting Mr Ryland-Hulme.'

93. 'I sum up.'

In this discussion very little individual expressive behaviour took place and the instances where it did are clearly recognized by the group in the subsequent analysis. It is agreed that the discussion as a whole was very much to the point, and very little concerned with morale-building, most of these latter contributions coming from the chairman. All the members were clear in their minds about the procedure in case-conferences, and since the problem itself was a single-step one—not containing a series of minor problems each of which has to be tackled before the next can be attempted—there was little discussion on procedure. The chairman was responsible for the order in which the points were put. The conference moved from information-exchange to proposals and agreement very nicely, Mr Carson being left out of it at the end. The group recognizes that each of the members was in his way an expert, and they also agree, a little belatedly, that the various experts had not respected each other as much as they might have done.

In answer to further questions the following points were covered:

Was there any 'unfreezing'? (laughter) No! Were all the points thrashed out properly? Mr Carson and Miss Smith deny this. The group concludes that if these two had made their points more clearly, the issues could have been thrashed out at greater length and there might then have been more unfreezing. On the whole, they are satisfied with the rate of progress; all members acknowledge that Mr Carson and Miss Smith seemed to hold up progress, but that the others did not listen very hard to what they wanted to say. Should there have been more definite proposals? No, the issues were clear.

Were the functions properly distributed among the members? This question is felt to be inappropriate, since here the roles were determined by the social groupings to which the members belonged. All now agree that the school-teacher was not sufficiently regarded. There was no need for additional experts, either from the group or from outside.

The group was interested, deeply involved and trying hard. It is agreed that the chairman and Miss Perry were the most co-operative, and that the others found it more difficult to keep out of competitive squabbles.

The group did not feel too dependent on anyone, and did not feel the need for more definite leadership. Miss Smith feels now that she was at times being left out of it, and the others agree that this had been so. All the members had been useful in the conference, and the group is able to acknowledge its own responsibility for the behaviour of those members who, at first sight, were not contributing to the good of the group. The group sees that it was most handicapped when dealing with members who had information and values which differed from their own.

For the sake of comparison, and as a fitting conclusion to the whole book, another recording ends this chapter. The right-hand side is kept blank for the reader to make his own comments. The students who took part in this discussion also had a social-work background. Their task was slightly more difficult, for they were to discuss the uses of the course in group work which they had just attended, and to suggest improvements. They are handicapped by having their instructor present, by having to reach agreement rather than come to an explicit decision, by having no clear role-structure, and by not dealing with the problem of procedure first. Mr Smith is a post-graduate student from the United States, and slightly older than the others. Mr Adidi is an African student who still has some language difficulties.

DISCUSSION ON GROUP WORK COURSE

Instructor: O.K.

(*long pause.*)

Mr Smith: Well, something has to be done here quick. (*laughter.*) Now we have before us this topic to find out our impressions of the course and what we think should be changed and what we liked about it, for the use of the people that come after us. Now I, for one, have no idea what a social worker really does and I don't speak correct English (*laughter*), so if some of the other people had some suggestions or ideas maybe they could educate me a little bit on this idea.

Miss Fynn: Mr Chairman, if I may speak. I should like to say that . . . er . . . this course has been invaluable in one or two ways, and that it helps us to . . . er . . . analyse what we are doing and saying in a constructive way and that we can by seeing our faults which I think we see quite plainly in these various lectures . . . We can improve . . . improve ourselves in some way. . . . I don't know what other people feel about that but I think it is invaluable in that way.

Miss Long: I think that for social workers who have committee work, I suppose most social workers will, it will be very useful. . . . What do you think? (*laughter.*)

Miss Mole: I should have said it is also useful for learning how to interview people, how to get them to say what you want them to say. I think these last role-playing recordings have been more useful than the first lectures, I think.

Miss Fynn: I think we couldn't have done role-playing without the first lectures.

Others: No, we wouldn't be able to.

Mr Adidi: Mr Chairman, I have been on this course but I don't know exactly what we intend today. Will you please explain what is the main purpose of the course?

READERS' COMMENTS

Mr Smith: I didn't know I was the chairman. (*laughter.*)
As I see it . . . the main purpose of the course was to
introduce you to some of the workings of a small group
and the interchange among people . . . how ideas are
presented back and forth. I remember at the beginning of
the course we analysed various conversations that had
taken place between, say, a worker and a boss, between
two men in a canteen . . . This kind of thing to see . . . the
basic structure of group-exchange, be it questioning, information seeking, things of this nature, so that we could
get an idea of how to analyse a conversation and with this
in mind you can tell something of the personality of the
person talking, his background, and then we worked it in
the latter part into role-playing, when we assumed a role
and tried to act out a situation that might occur in life to
the social worker . . . if you had an interview with a person
who came to you for relief . . . or something of that nature.

Miss Fynn: In this business of role-playing, how far do you
think that our own characters have come out in the attempt
to play another character?

Miss Long: I don't think we really got into the characters.

Miss Mole: Too self-conscious.

Mr Smith: What do you think about role-playing as such . . .?
Do you think that the people that play the roles should
know more about them . . . should have done some more
work on it?

Miss Mole: Yes, I think so, and also I think that the group is
rather large . . . for people not to be self-conscious . . . and
people do not know each other.

Miss Long: But I think we have got over that a lot, haven't we?
(*long pause and some laughter.*)

Mr Smith: In other words, you have got one suggestion, that
the group is too large?

Miss Mole: Yes, I think so.

Mr Smith: And the second one that we should do a little
bit more work before you play the role?

Miss Mole: ⎫
Miss Long: ⎬ Yes.

Mr Smith: At least the two people get together a little bit more.

Miss Mole: But you can't get together because in real life you never know what the other person's going to say, do you, or much about them?

Mr Smith: Well, if you . . . Does someone else have any idea on this?

Miss Fynn: It has been said that if you are suddenly presented with a personality that you have to form an opinion about pretty quickly, you have to have some time to think what the person's reactions would be in the same sort of situations. I mean, obviously they would be different from your own and if you have got to do it immediately then your own reactions are going to come over rather than what you think the person would say. Do you know what I mean?

Mr Smith: Er, in other words . . .

Miss Long: Except that they are . . .

Mr Smith: What you are trying to say is that you have to live the part of the person you are portraying?

Miss Fynn: Yes.

Mr Smith: Remember the problems we got into with that school situation where we . . . they weren't sure whether it was a boy or girl they were talking about and deciding how old the child was. . . . I think you are trying to say that if you had the part you were going to play maybe a week in advance and you didn't talk to the other person . . . but at least you had something in common. You knew what the situation was . . . it might have worked a little bit better.

Mr Adidi: I think that apart from role-playing we have to consider other factors which . . . could make a successful committee meeting. . . . I would consider the place of the

chairman as a very important one. I think the success of any meeting depends upon the role of the chairman. I think we have to consider that too. . . .

Mr Smith: How would you consider it . . . the role of a chairman? How would you go about teaching this then?

Mr Adidi: Well, I think he has to be someone who knows something about the subject going to be discussed and he should have wider capabilities.

Mr Smith: You mean you would rather see one of the students perhaps chairman a discussion at times to gain experience?

Mr Adidi: Certainly. . . . If you are going to conduct any discussion you want someone to lead the meeting and I think as the leader he should be well versed in the topic that will be discussed.

Miss Long: Yes, but the function of this course has been that it teaches us all the different types of roles, to show us not just the chairman but ordinary members' roles. (*small pause.*)

Mr Smith: Everyone looks at their watches. (*laughter.*) Have you got an idea, I . . . I . . . don't quite get what you are driving at. Because we have studied committees and we have studied the personality that was the chairman . . . actually all our meetings have been chairmanned by one person . . . Now would you suggest . . . if I read your mind right you suggest having us at times take over a meeting and . . . and try our hand at it?

Mr Adidi: What I am saying is that all the time we have been considering role-playing and I think it is not the only aspect of the committee meeting or whatever meeting you might have. I think there are other aspects . . . I consider the role of the chairman very important.

Miss Fynn: May I say that I think this is . . . this sort of thing is very good? I wish we had more of it because in social work, the very essence of social work is that people have some give-and-take and that a social worker can't work merely on his own, he has to sort of know other people's

opinions . . . when you are working with people you work with . . . and it teaches you to work as a group. This sort of thing which we haven't had before . . . more than two people. As far as social work is concerned, I think this is very good.

Mr Smith: Well, would you like to say, instead of role-playing with two people, role-playing like we are doing now, with six?

Omnes: Yes.

Mr Smith: Have you ever had a course in how to lead a conference?

Omnes: No.

Mr Smith: As one of the courses, in other words . . .

Miss Fynn: Are there such things in American universities?

Mr Smith: There are courses given in group-leadership, as such. It is under a different title but I just wondered if you had a course of this nature here.

Miss Mole: No.

Mr Adidi: I think this is the first of this kind.

Mr Smith: This course is the first of its kind here?

Miss Fynn: I think it would be awfully good particularly for club-leaders. I mean . . . now . . . they're just sort of thrust into crowds of bawling children and haven't much sort of background of how to deal with them.

Miss Mole: I was thinking of things more like case-conferences or . . . something like that.

Others: Yes.

Miss Mole: . . . where you have got to give something constructive and work with people—the other people.

Mr Smith: What do you run up against in these case-problems in your work? As I understand you you are out part of the time with social workers, aren't you? . . .

Miss Long: Yes, but then we bring back and discuss with all the other people concerned in the case, that is the ideal.

Miss Mole: That's the ideal.

Mr Smith: Yes, I see; well, could you bring back one of these cases, say, and work it out as a group for us in this course?

Miss Fynn: Yes.

Miss Mole: We could, I suppose.

Miss Long: Yes.

Miss Fynn: That would be an excellent idea.

Miss Mole: And each be a different kind of social worker all round. (*laughter.*)

Mr Smith: You could have yourselves as separate people to make the judgment and have a couple of people act out a social case, and you have to give your opinions and views on it. . . . We are supposed to be coming to three concrete suggestions . . . so that we can get rid of this microphone. (*laughter.*)
We have had, let's see, how many? . . . We have had one about making the class smaller. Two—your idea of . . .

Mr Adidi: Responsibility.

Mr Smith: Response to . . . er . . . switching the role of chairmanship round so that others get a chance at it. Three—the idea of training to be chairman, which is, I take it, the same kind of thing. I think the two of you are about in agreement, aren't you?

Mr Adidi: And about the duration of the course. I understand that this is going to be a ten weeks' course. I wonder if that is sufficient for us to know all that we would like to know about groups.

Mr Smith: What do you do next term . . .⎫
Miss Mole: It probably isn't . . .⎬
                                    ⎭

Miss Fynn: Perhaps we are meant to be stimulated by the course. (*laughter.*)

15

CONCLUSION

In what respects can this book be said to have contributed to an understanding of the principles underlying decision-making? The general answer is that a set of words has been introduced, in terms of which the experience of making decisions in groups can be more adequately described. An intuitive understanding of group-processes can thereby be made communicable to others: through the use of these words, vague impressions can be brought into the daylight to be examined and approved, or criticized and corrected.

For instance, it is common knowledge that groups exist in a wider social context. But it has been enlightening to analyse, in detail, the effect of this context on the functioning of the members: on consultation, on responsibility, on personal relations. Similarly, the fact that a large part of any man's stock of ideas derives from the daily contacts which everyone takes for granted gives point to the insistence that relevant groups must participate in the preliminaries to a decision that will affect them.

Our analysis was able to take account of the information which is available to the group, whether or not it is equally distributed among the members; of the ways in which proposals emerge from this information; of the factors, rational and emotional, which will affect the final agreement. By applying this analysis to the internal structure of the group it was possible to show how decisions may be handicapped by rigid and erroneous distinctions between leadership (or chairmanship) and membership. An analysis of the logical sequence of interaction when decisions are being made clarified the functions of members, since the proper exercise of their functions should show itself in an interaction-structure suited to the current task. A consideration of the task threw light on the desirability of strong leadership as contrasted with full participation by all members.

Through an understanding of the relation between the demands of the task and the functions of members, the concept of 'roles' was introduced. The later part of the book could, therefore, be devoted to the effects of ill-defined or inappropriate—as well as of rationally ideal—role-structures. This in turn led to the consideration of real-life examples of members learning to perform the roles suitable to particular tasks. Role-playing was introduced as a technique for creating a variety of circumstances in which newly-learnt skills may be applied, and group self-evaluation gives the group an instrument with which these lessons may be hammered home. For the danger is that the learning may be at one remove: that practice in analysis may not go hand in hand with improvement in skills. It requires knowledge and discipline to play the appropriate roles in a whole variety of different settings, to confine oneself mainly to the relevant but to be expressive when the occasion demands it, to listen to one's own contributions with the same detachment with which one listens to others, and to correct one's own faults with the alacrity with which one notices those of others.

INDEX

Authors' names are indexed also to pages where their work has a bearing on the arguments or findings to which the text refers.

237